MW01625926

"…the time when I first set eyes upon the glorious woman
of my mind, who was known to many as Beatrice…
She came clad in vermilion, the noblest color, modest and virtuous;
girdled and adorned in harmony with her tender years."

Dante Alighieri, *La Vita Nuova*

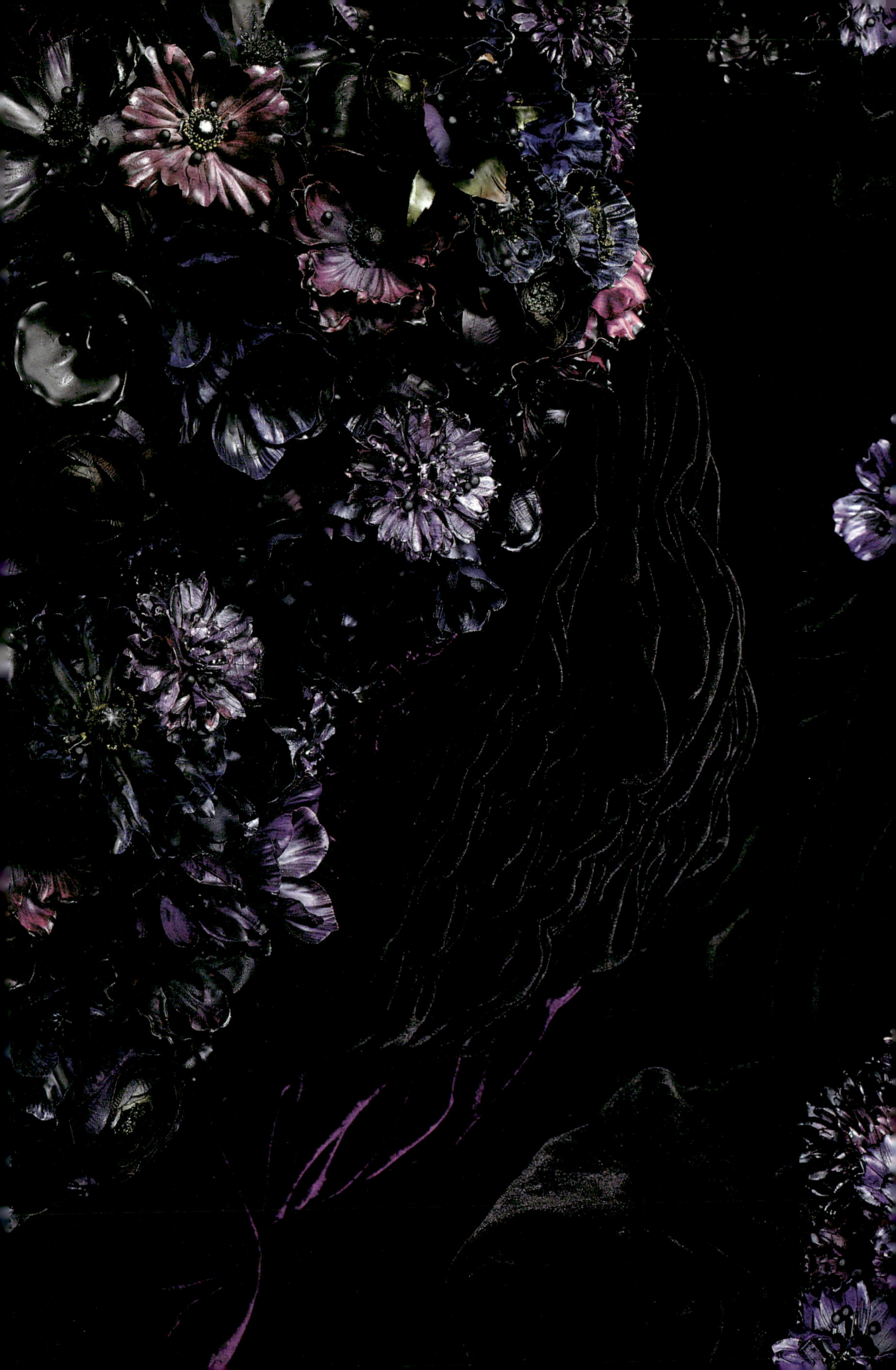

Petah Coyne
vermilion fog

CHARTA

GALERIE LELONG

Contents

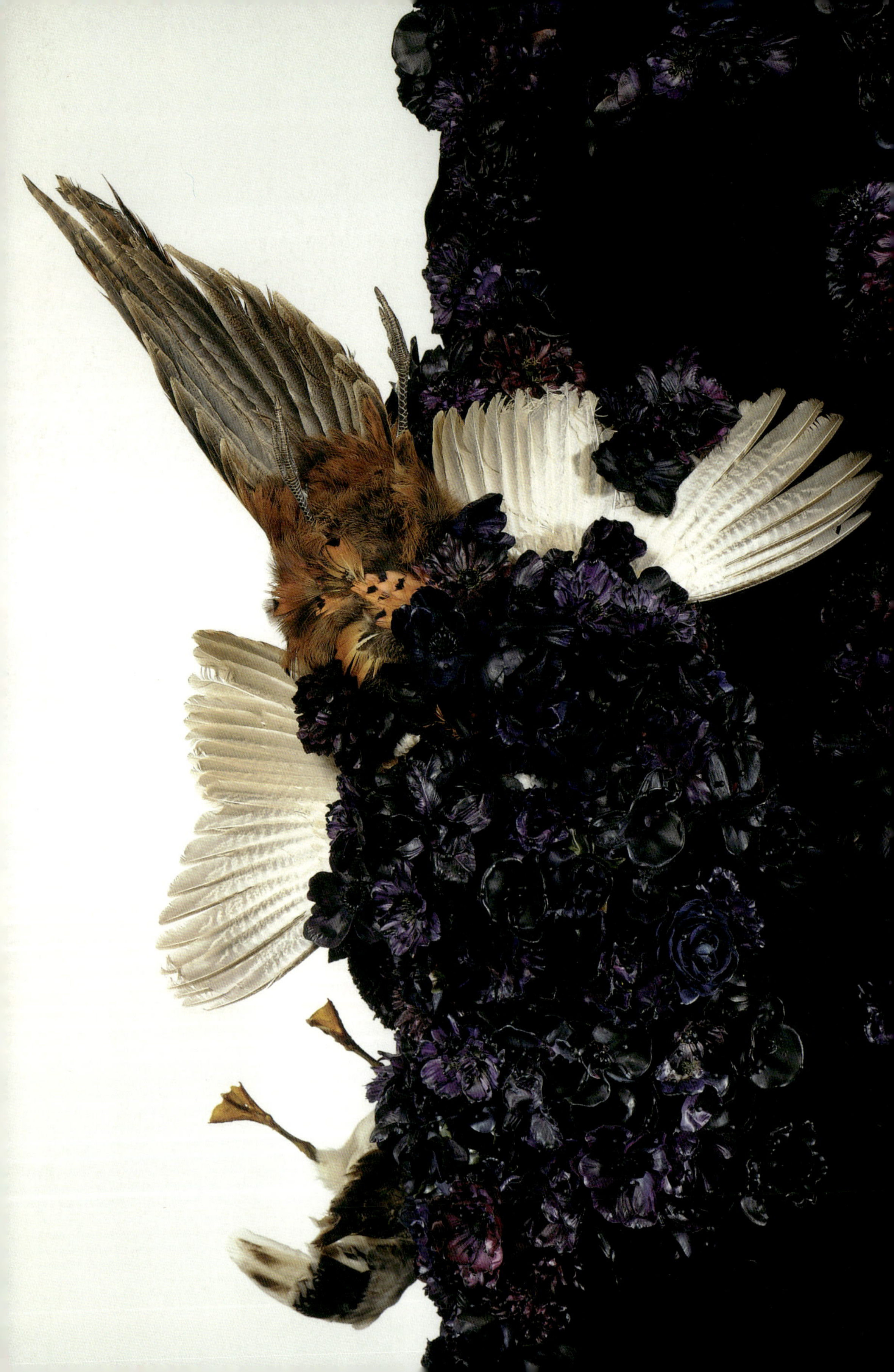

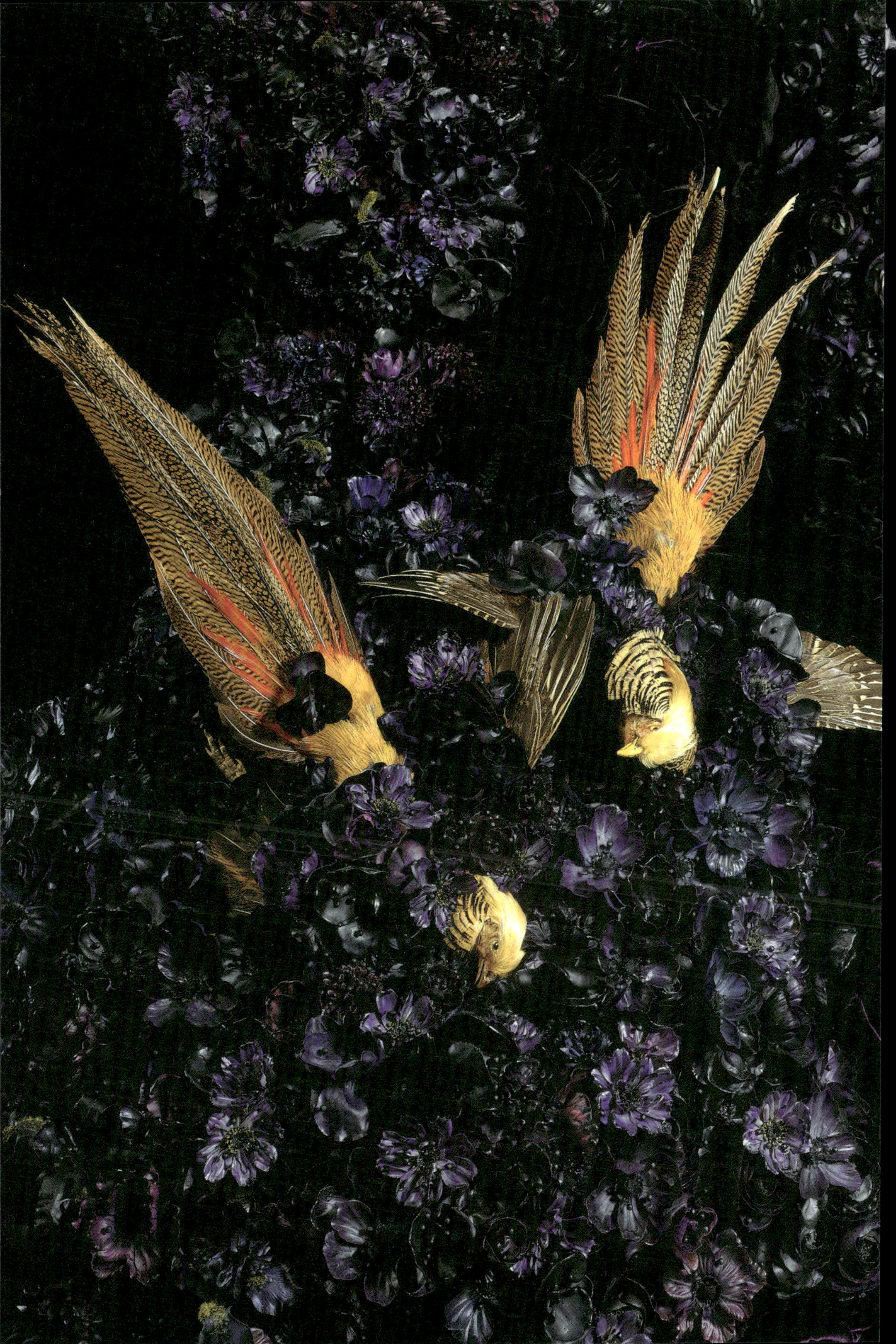

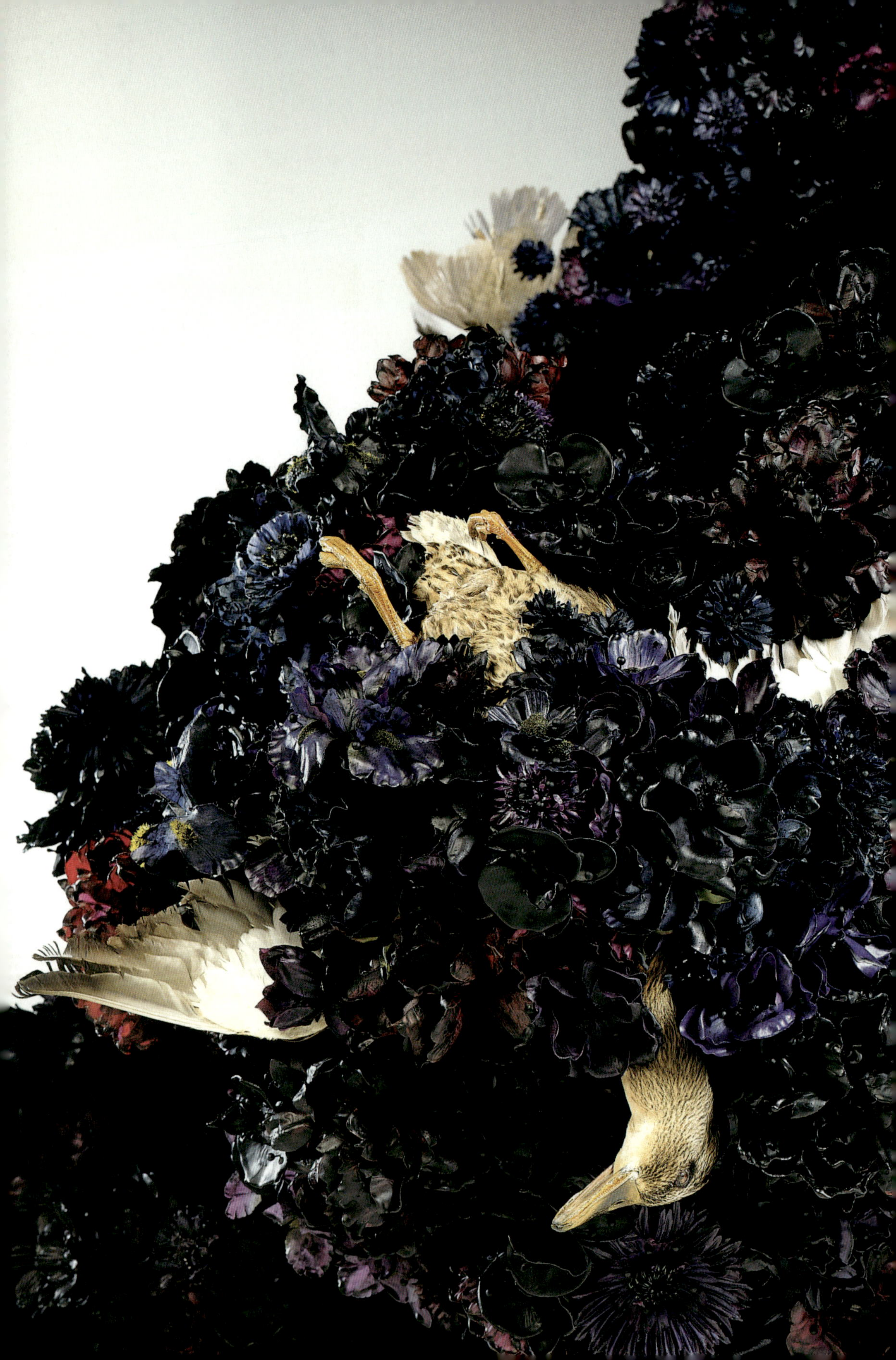

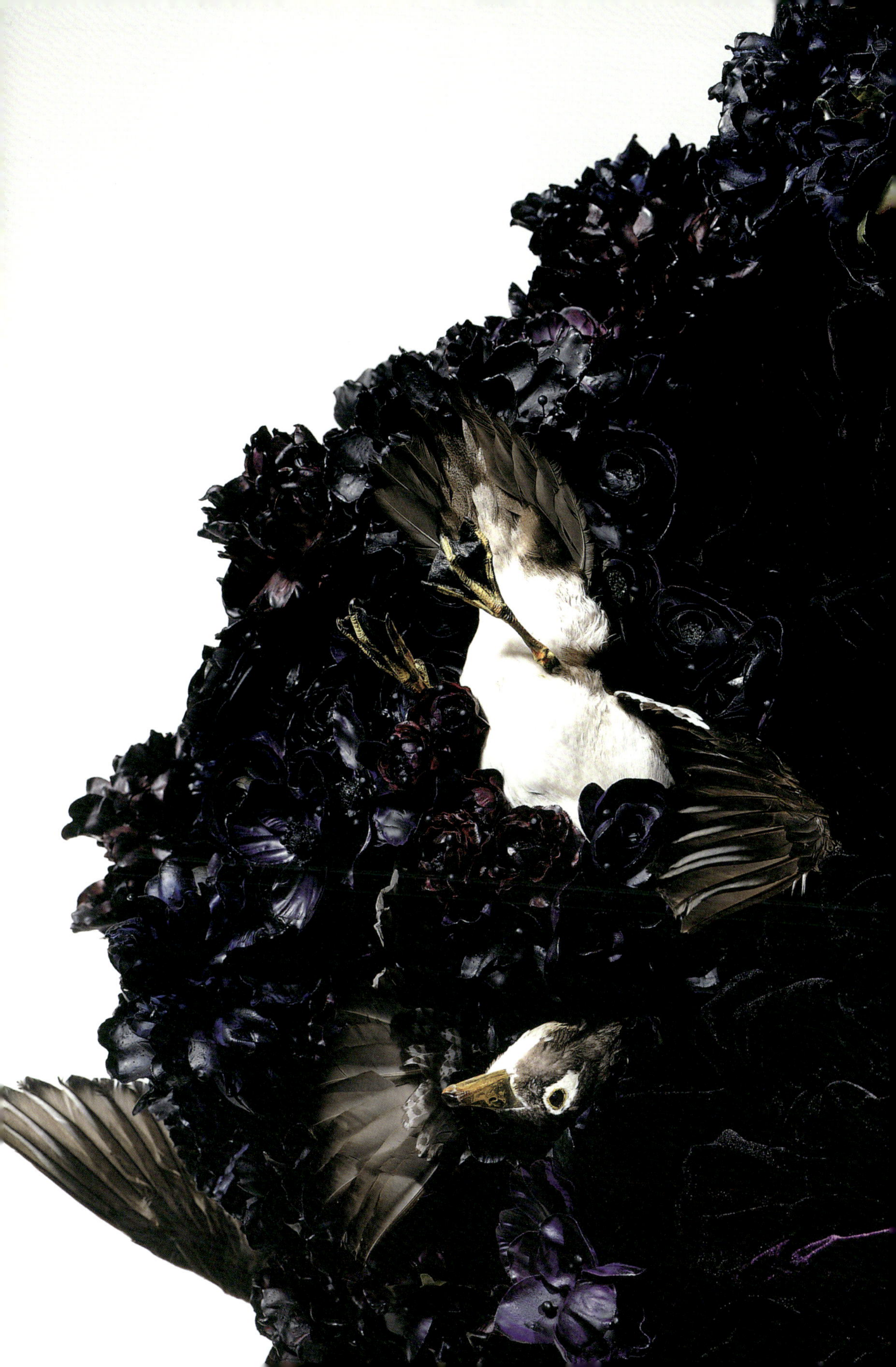

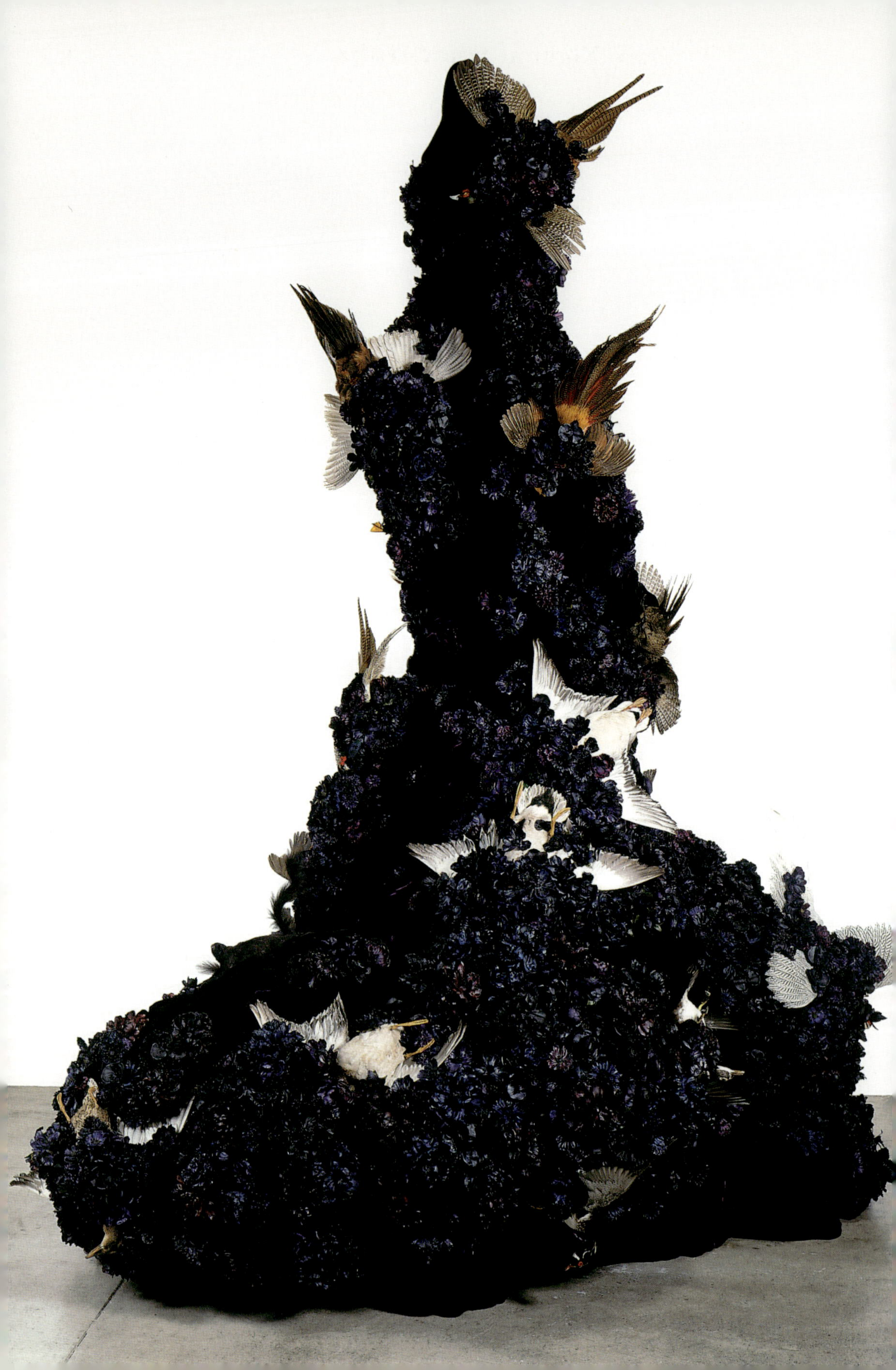

Dark Night at Heart's Lake

Ann Wilson Lloyd

The Water Temple, Tadao Ando's partially submerged Buddhist temple in Japan,[1] is entered through a deep, narrow stairwell. The descent slices through a circular lily pond covering the temple's roof, and except for this watery crown, the building's exterior is all smooth, gray, minimalist forms—curved concrete walls, gravel paths, steel railings—directing the visitor below. There, following a winding course to the innermost sanctum of the Buddha statue, one is gradually bathed in saturated vermilion light. Its intensity increases toward dusk, courtesy of the dying sun.

Petah Coyne visited the Water Temple while on a six-month Asian Cultural Council fellowship to Japan in 1992–93. The experience was eidetic:

"You walk down and you know you're under the pond. You feel the pressure, but it's also a kind of release in a certain way. I remember lying on the floor—there was nobody else there. It's the most intense, beautiful space.

Vermilion is the color Japanese use for their Buddhist temples. That color, all those pillars, the staring and meditating, it seems to me sends the monks into a vermilion fog, another world, somewhere between this world and the next—or maybe between this world and a more imperfect world.

We crossed over to the temple island in a boat. It had been very foggy, and the area was very near the epicenter of the earthquake that happened later. I remember thinking then that this would be the perfect place for the Inferno to open up."[2]

Perhaps a netherworld did crack open for Coyne back then. From somewhere deep in her artistic psyche, a host of dramatic black works

Untitled #1180 (Beatrice), 2003–08

has come steadily marching in the past decade or so. Darkness of course has long been the flip side of her repertoire; her huge, hanging, tuberous works[3] from the late 1980s and early 1990s, soaked in motor oil and covered with gritty black sand, were blackness (and black humor) made manifest. Earlier works paid noir-ish homage to death and resurrection. *Fish Lines*, 1979–83, *Fish Room*, 1982, and *Fish Tree*, 1983,[4] all contained seafood from Chinatown fish markets that Coyne embalmed with resin and suspended inside and outside her SoHo loft.

Since her visit to the Water Temple, these themes are guised in Victorian and neo-Gothic blends of the funereal, the decorative and the decadent. The sad, gorgeous, bride-like *Paris Blue*[5] and the morphing *Daphne* (both 2002–03), for instance, are larger-than-life, figurative

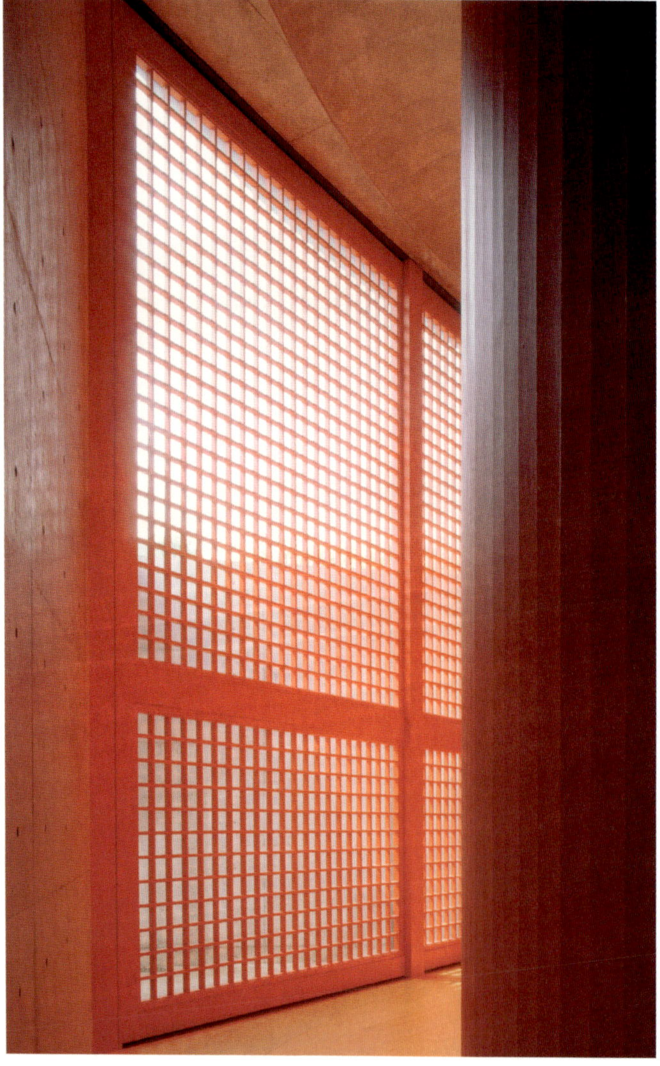

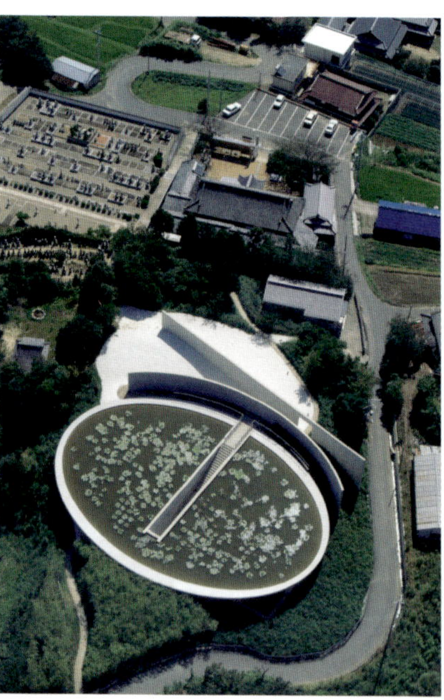

Tadao Ando, Water Temple (Shingonshu Hompukuji), 1991. Awaji-shima Island, Hyōgo Prefecture, Japan Courtesy Tadao Ando Architect & Associates

forms costumed in ravishing, haute couture gown-like formations of dark wax, dyed silk flowers, tassels and feathers among other things. In the very latest works, this material richness expands with satin and velvet and is accessorized with unlikely additions. Sometimes somber only in spirit, other times in color, too, these drop-dead gorgeous manifestations are slowly emerging as the cast of an epic narrative.

If the most recent works have stepped from Coyne's own vermilion fog, on a more worldly level, this exhibition's title and theme are also based on the transporting experience of film and literature. Narrative metaphor has always been an important (though not often noted) source for her. This installation in particular—with separate rooms and lacy scrim dividing the two—is meant to invoke the cinematic experience of entering a place emotionally and perceptually, but not physically. In Coyne's mind, the larger, attainable, mostly dark room represents hell, or possibly hell on earth, hence its designation as *Dante's Inferno.* The unattainable, mostly white room is purgatory, or, it could be heaven, or just somewhere generally better. Whatever, she's titled it *Unforgiven,* referring to the 1992 Clint Eastwood western about frontier revenge and redemption.

The curtain between them evolved from Coyne's many visits to sacred places, where grids or screens fence off the holiest spaces and objects.[6] She also mentions The Metropolitan Museum of Art's roped off period rooms, and house museums (like the Isabella Stewart Gardner Museum in Boston) where vintage fabrics like lace, silk wall coverings and draperies are displayed as art.

Here, the *Unforgiven* works, at which one can only gaze, suggest suspended souls, neither here nor there. Neither is it for us to know if the white confections of signature wax, feathers, velvet, ribbons, silk leaves, flowers and birds, are stopped in the act of ascending or descending.

Frosty and pristine at first take, their sagging shapes and encrusted details slowly convey what the artist calls "the beauty of sadness, a very Japanese idea." They are feminine in form—suggestive of bonnets, bouquets or skirts—but their layered delicacy has been accreted almost to the breaking point. Their stiff metal armaments sag floorward. Blossoms droop under thick pearly shrouds. Fragile birds struggle against wax prisons. Scattered petals on the floor suggest entropy. These are elegiac tributes to victims of hubris, lost causes, moral dilemmas and thwarted lives.

Tetiaroa, 2007, is named after the Tahitian atoll owned by Marlon Brando, whose fame eventually corrupted his own paradise. *Secret Life of Words*, 2007, takes its name from the 2005 Tim Robbins movie about a war-ravaged female Bosnian refugee. *Late Spring*, 2007–08, pays homage to the 1949 film by Yasujiro Ozu about a daughter duty-bound to her widowed father. *Night Mother*, 2007–08, references the 1980s play and film (*'night, Mother*) about a daughter's heartbreakingly rational suicide.

Three black works in this room counterpoint the poignancy. Hand-tailored velvet shrouds extinguish chandeliers *Death in Venice* and *Playtime*, both 2003-08. Their elegance trails into tatters, or sprouts feathery collars of decadence and frivolity. *Playtime*, named for the 1967 Jacques Tati satire of modern conformity, is caught in the act of going Goth. *Death in Venice*, after the Thomas Mann morality tale, seems to have danced too long at *carnevale*. Even so, they are *luxe*, desirable things, a perfect blend of the fanciful and licentious.

The more serious *Raise the Red Lantern*, 2007–08, bundles sensual pleasure with pain. This inverted bouquet of black and red takes its name from the visually lush but tragic 1991 Zhang Yimou film about domestic treachery. Coyne's sculpture is bristling and sloughing; prick-

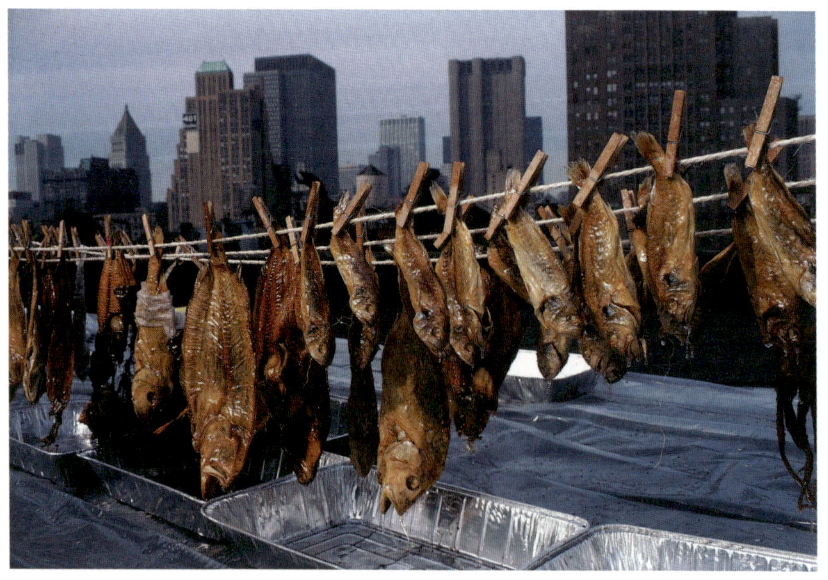

Fish Lines, 1979–1983. Dead fish, squid, octopus, baby barracuda, rope, resin. Rooftop view, Broome Street, New York

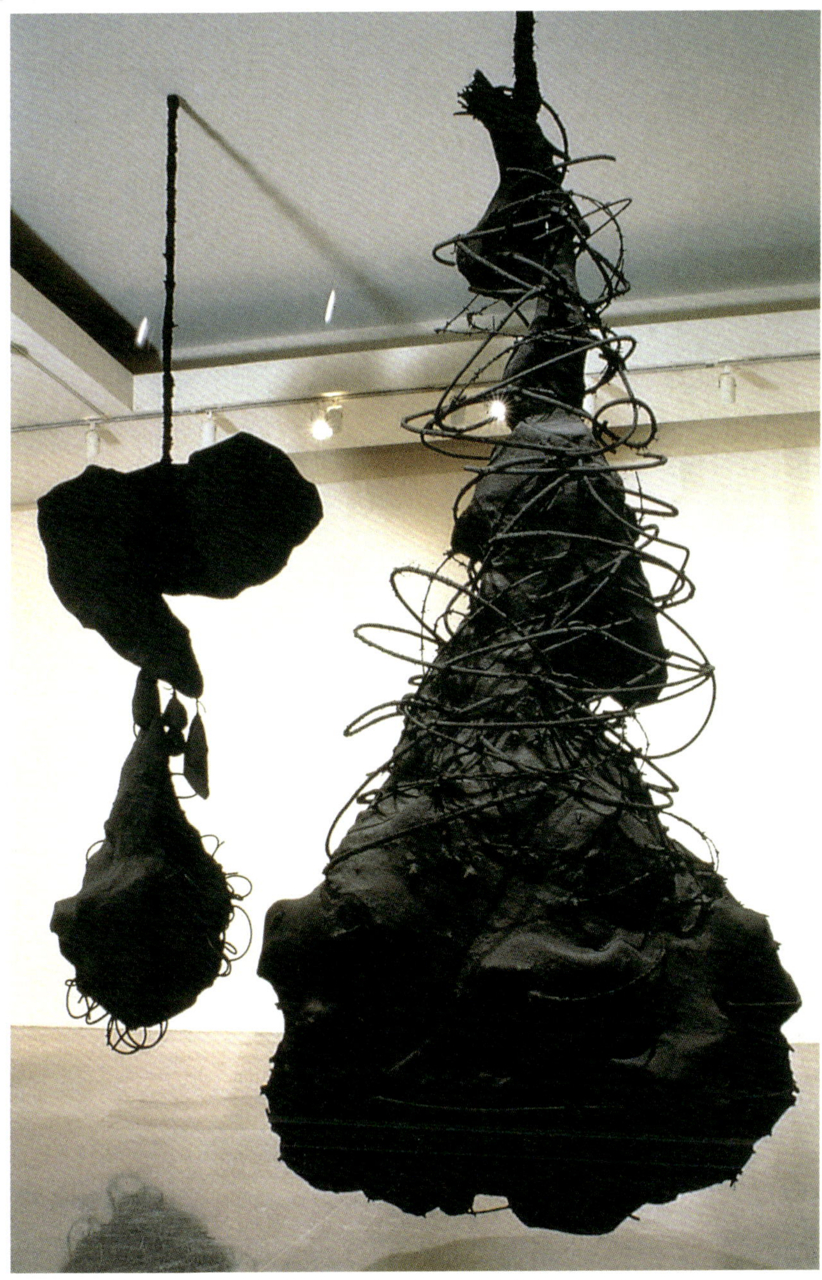

Untitled Installation: A Grand Lobby Project, Brooklyn Museum, New York, 1989. Photo: K. McCarthy

ly pinecones, barely visible, are embedded among the roses and ranunculus. In tribute to the film's lovely Chinese heroine who's betrayed in conjugal games, its excoriating beauty, like that of the red lantern's, is a signal of doom.

> *"Then I could feel the terror begin to ease*
> *That churned in my heart's lake all through the night."*
>
> Canto I, Dante's *Inferno*[7]

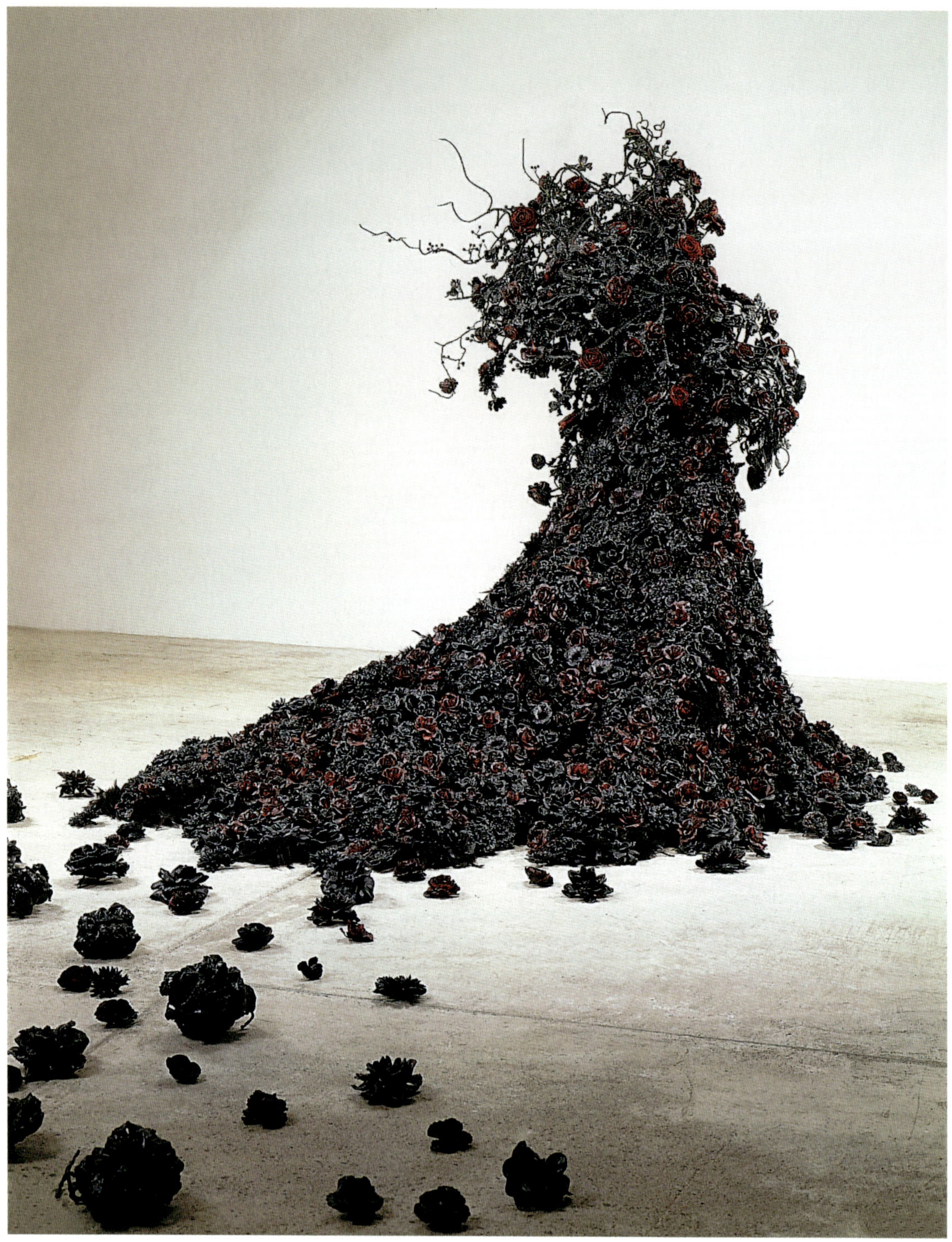

Untitled #1103 (Daphne), 2002–03
Wax statuary with human and horse hair, silk flowers, wired tree branches, curly willow branches, bows, acetate ribbon, tassels, feathers, fabricated rubber, specially formulated wax, pigment, black spray paint, pearl-headed hatpins, chicken wire fencing, wire, acrylic primer, plywood, metal hardware
77 x 83 x 86 inches (194.8 x 209.9 x 217.6 cm)
Collection of Julie and John Thornton

Outside the curtain it's another story—one that Coyne has her own take on:

"Dante's Inferno *is very much about the personal and the public, what happens to all of us. The imagery is so beautiful, the descent into the concentric circles, all those trapdoors. Each soul appears, tells his or her own individual story and dives back into their own dark hole."*

In the fourteenth century, men of science ascribed the flow of unbridled passions, fear and anxiety to an actual source in the human heart called the "heart's lake."[8] In the heart of Coyne's dark works, it's still nighttime at the lake, and the waters roil.

Literary nuance, due only in part to subtitles, underlies her most recent work. Like Dante's *Inferno*, Coyne's newest sculptures are dense, surreal, tangled, vivid with metaphor and, most obviously to date, rich with animal imagery. Creatures large and small lurk within and around them, without turning these complex constructions into mere background. The works' Stygian darkness might glimmer with deep, glowing hues, like vermilion and purple; they might shift from ordinary human scale to that of landscape or nightmare. Yet even at their most metamorphic they are more of the earth (or below it), less celestial than the pristine white works.

Realism via taxidermy bird and mammal specimens supports this reading. *Virgil*, 1997-2008, a copse of charred-looking woodland with hidden fauna imprisoned in thick flora, feels diorama-like. The flowers here have a different sheen, like the bruised and inky iridescence inside mussel shells. Over a dozen once-living things are tucked inside, including a bobcat, which Coyne perceives as Virgil, leading a large game bird, which she thinks of as Dante. Close looking also reveals a black squirrel, a pair of smaller birds, and other creatures.

In Dante's day, woods were dreaded places, their wild inhabitants likened to the beasts within untamed hearts. Birds, however—from Egyptian tomb painting to Giotto's depictions of St. Francis—have been assigned loftier roles as escorts to the afterlife or departing souls themselves. In Coyne's work (as in Dante's) animal imagery in general should not be read as specific allusions, but cumulatively, for overall effect.

Aside from moral or religious metaphors, even in this day of ecological awareness, that effect is often colored by our ineffable response to real animals. Coyne ascribes her creatures empathetic roles, even pays homage to their sad remains, but also admits that live animals seem a bit alien to her. Some viewers, meanwhile, might recoil from these dead bodies, while others sorrow over so much wasted beauty. Proud hunters or taxidermists (who rightly consider themselves artists of a kind) might even be offended at liberties taken. Across the spectrum of response, dead creatures continue to emit charges to our own live nerve endings.

There's a connection, too, between these stuffed specimens and objects, like religious statues, that have often acted as a generative heart in Coyne's work. Frequently, she has hidden or buried things within the sculptures—a psychic irritant, a treasured keepsake or symbolic icon—which then acts like the oyster's proverbial grain of sand.

As with the pearl, these objects become so accreted they are frequently nullified, or nearly so, but always transformed. Sometimes they're kept secret, sometimes not. Aside from any personal exorcism, of course, Coyne's work stems equally from her irrepressible and unique esthetic, her affinity for haptic, seductive materials and an ever-present formalist acuity. But there is also the possibility that these buried objects are simply too tender to be left exposed—that work must be made for and from them.

Black Cloud and *Tom's Twin*, both 2007-08, have each grown organically from now-obscured sources, becoming lavish, dramatic 3-D Rorschachs. *Tom's Twin*, with its dark-shrouded chandelier, looks both grave and gravid. It harbors an heirloom baby crib from Coyne's family within its beautiful red-tinged tumulus. *Black Cloud* contains a female statue. Both these funereal works calls up rampant floral casket sprays, burned gardens, oil spills, lava flows, or a fallen figure in an extravagant gown. Anna Karenina on the tracks, perhaps?

Meanwhile *Camel's Back*, 2005–07, is more subtly allusive and surreal. Vaguely bird-like in form, it's also an elaborate Victorian bouquet, one that's been yanked directly from the soil. Despite its elegant artifice, tender taproots left dangling toward the floor are the loveliest part.

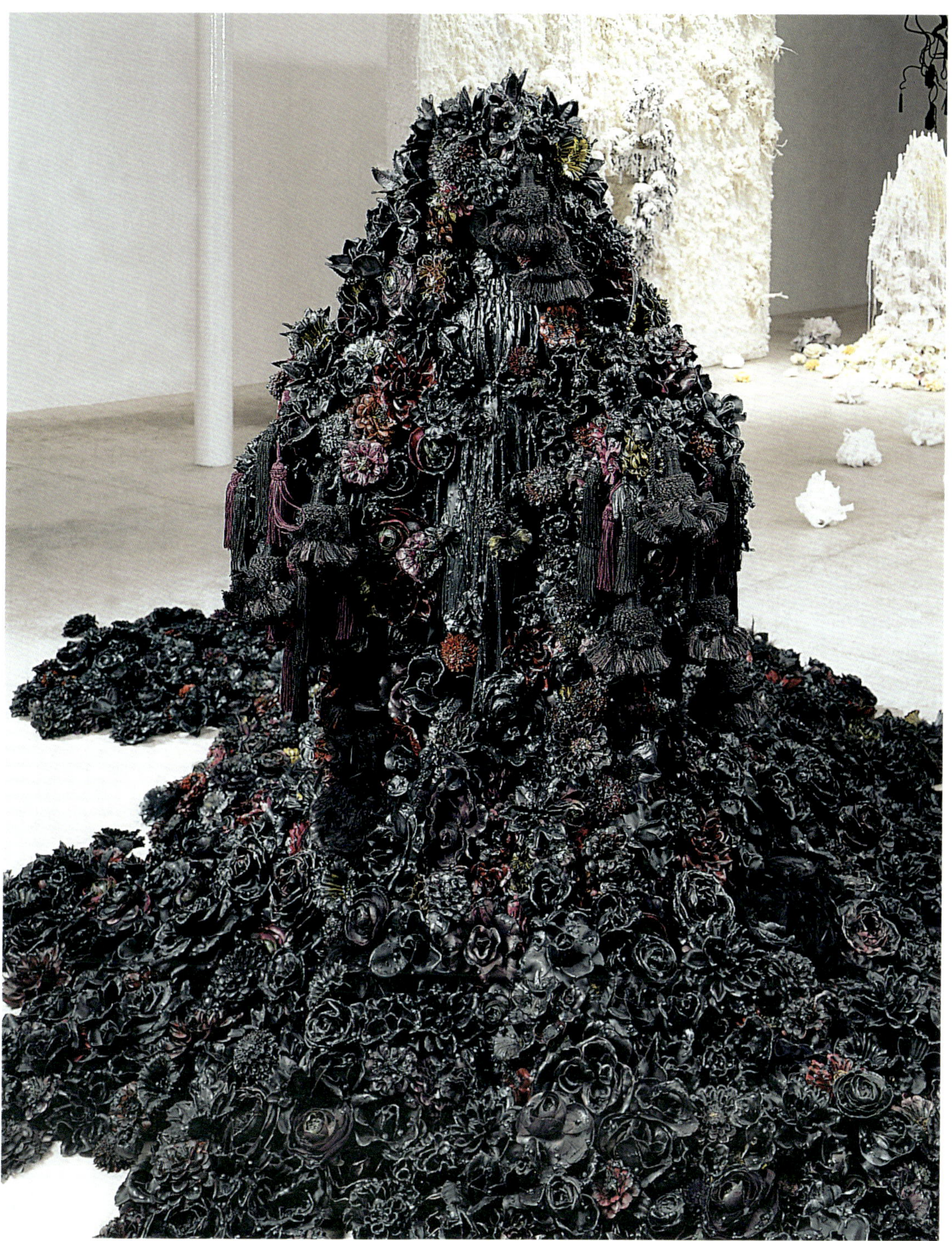

Untitled #1165 (Paris Blue), 2002–03
Wax statuary, silk flowers, bows, tassels, acetate ribbon, feathers, specially formulated wax, pigment, chicken wire fencing, pearl-headed hatpins, acrylic paint, acrylic primer, wood, plywood, metal hardware
51 x 132 x 168 inches
(129 x 333.9 x 425 cm)

Collection Joslyn Art Museum, Omaha, Nebraska
Museum Purchase with Funds Provided by Richard and Mary Holland, 2003

"...the time when I first set eyes upon the glorious woman
of my mind, who was known to many as Beatrice...
She came clad in vermilion, the noblest color, modest and virtuous;
girdled and adorned in harmony with her tender years."

Dante Alighieri, *La Vita Nuova*

Coyne's *Beatrice*, 2003-08, comes clad not in vermilion, but caught, perhaps, in her own patch of transformative vermilion fog. Every element in this piece is in a state of transience, thrusting up, tumbling down. Though her form rises like a peak in a Chinese landscape painting, the winged creatures that ought to lift this spirit drag on it instead. They are literally exquisite corpses, half bird, half botanical, as they merge the unfaded glory of their feathers with those deep purple-black blooms and branches.

More than previous figurative works, *Beatrice* is treated to lavish passages of the dressmaker's art. Swaths of ruched purple and black velvet simulate thick, dark waters that swirl around her like a vortex—as if she's rising from the depths of the Inferno's charnel lakes. (Coyne says she can't help thinking of the flows and eddies of the fluid velvet as "spills of blood, pooling in front of her.")

But those birds, their brilliant plumage, their downy white bellies, their little orange feet sticking ludicrously skyward, are what has stopped *Beatrice*, and us, in our respective tracks. Some underground force, some dark disaster-dream has happened here, and within the folds of *Beatrice's* skirt, three small black squirrels bear witness. The whole ensemble is a bit unnerving. Should all who set eyes on this version of Dante's glorious woman abandon hope?

Not exactly. For despite *Beatrice's* creepy, astonishing fabulousness, she is also a bit like a Victorian lady's chapeau gone seriously wrong. Measures of irony and black humor hone Coyne's ability to finesse the seriously dead and never alive into awesome, feral beauty, and endow each supremely exquisite creation with a touch of the absurd. Hell on earth, that inevitable dark storm that comes to churn the lake of the heart, is made bearable by cultivating a precise blend of wryness and fortitude, and then making astounding work from it—an epic poem, an epic body of sculpture—all aiming at the rosy glow of another, better world.

No longer striking fear, today Dante's nine circles of hell are often employed as mere figurative fun. One could surmise that Coyne's brilliantly mad and harrowing methods must send her there and back on a daily basis. The sheer craziness of piling up tens of thousands of quadruple-wax-dipped silk flowers and every dead, stuffed animal she can get her hands on spins an alternate narrative that ultimately can sound like a dark, absurdist comedy. But it is also divine, and deeply human.

1. Tadao Ando's 1991 Hompukuji Temple, known as the Water Temple, is on Awaji-shima Island, Japan.
2. All quotes from Petah Coyne are from conversations with the author in 2008.
3. See Douglas Dreishpoon, "The Still Point of Time," essay in *Petah Coyne: Above and Beneath the Skin*, exhibition catalogue, Albright-Knox Art Gallery, Buffalo, New York, 2005, pp. 26–32.
4. Ibid. pp. 16–18.
5. Coyne's more recent works are mostly untitled but numbered, with subtitles in parentheses, i.e., *Paris Blue* is actually *Untitled #1165 (Paris Blue)*. From here in the text, all further titles are abbreviated to their subtitles.
6. Specifically, she mentions the vermilion grid wall deep inside Ando's Water Temple, and the same device in saffron used by Luis Barragán in his chapel, the Capuchinas Sacramentarias del Purisimo Corazón de Maria, in Mexico City.
7. *The Inferno of Dante*, translated by Robert Pinsky, with notes by Nicole Pinsky, Farrar, Straus and Giroux, New York, 1994, p. 5.
8. Ibid., Nicole Pinsky, p. 378.
9. Umberto Eco, ed., quoted in *History of Beauty*, Rizzoli, New York, 2004, p. 171

Dante's Inferno

pp. 25, 27 **Untitled #1203 (Camel's Back)**, 2005–07

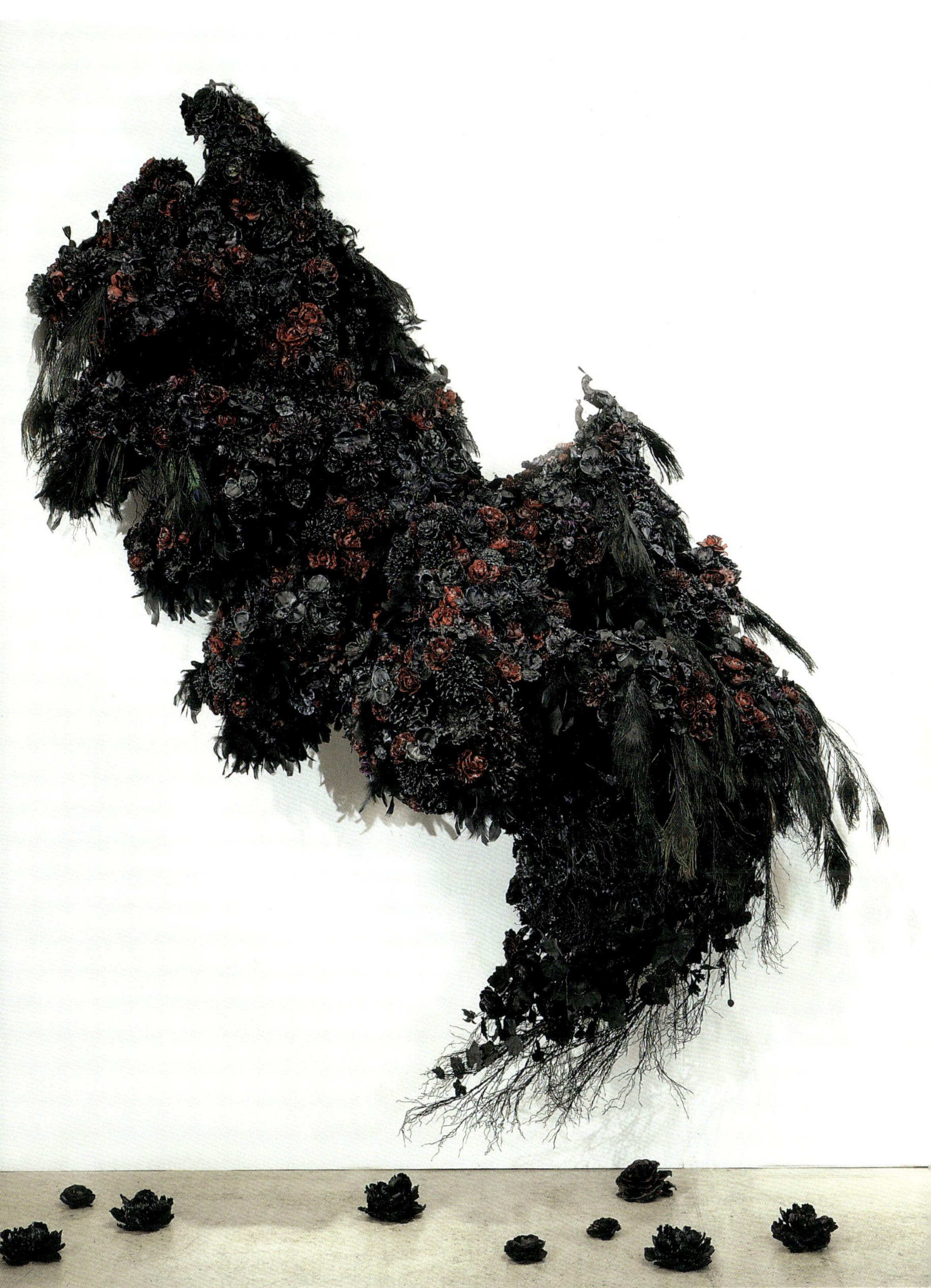

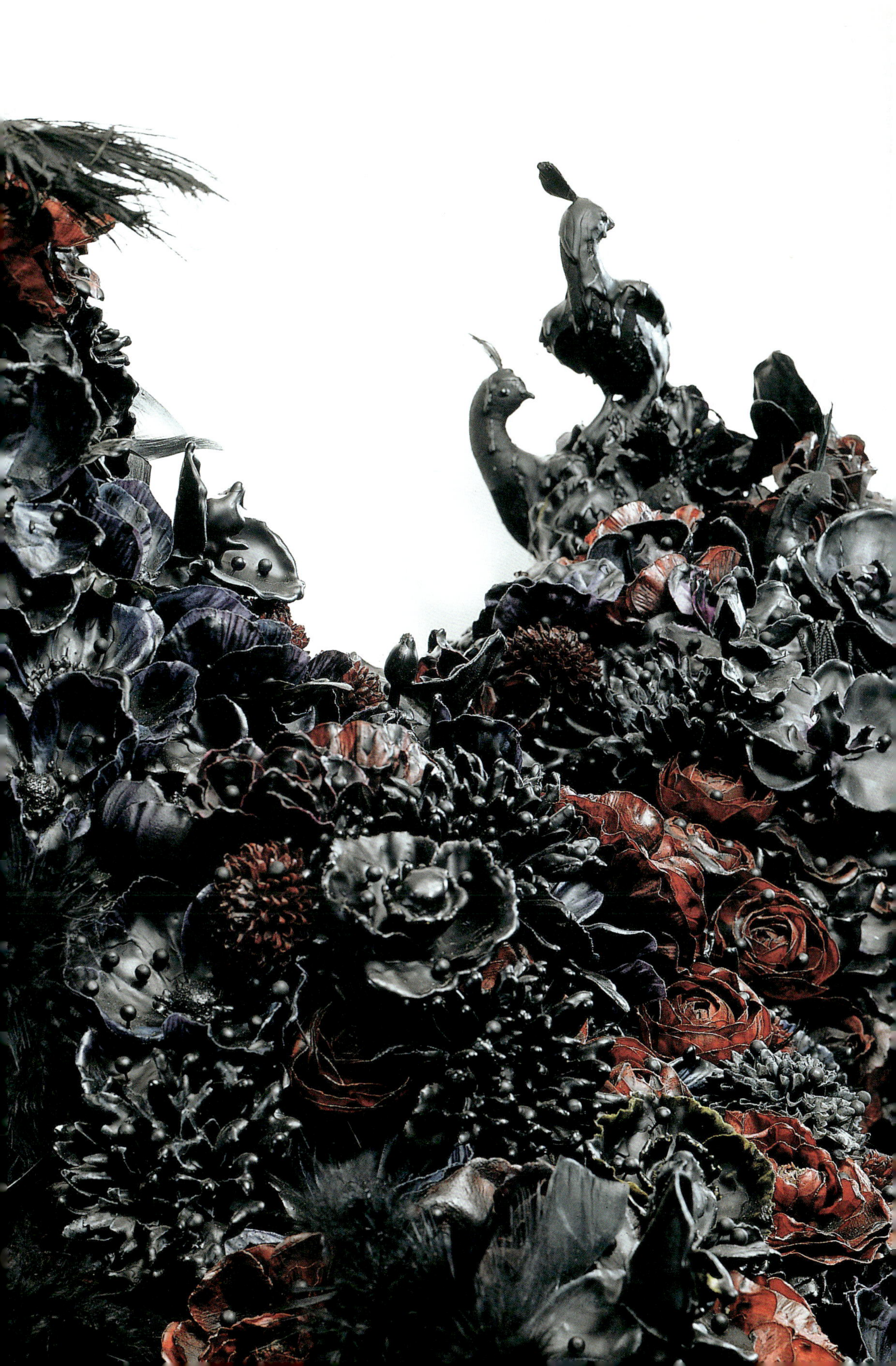

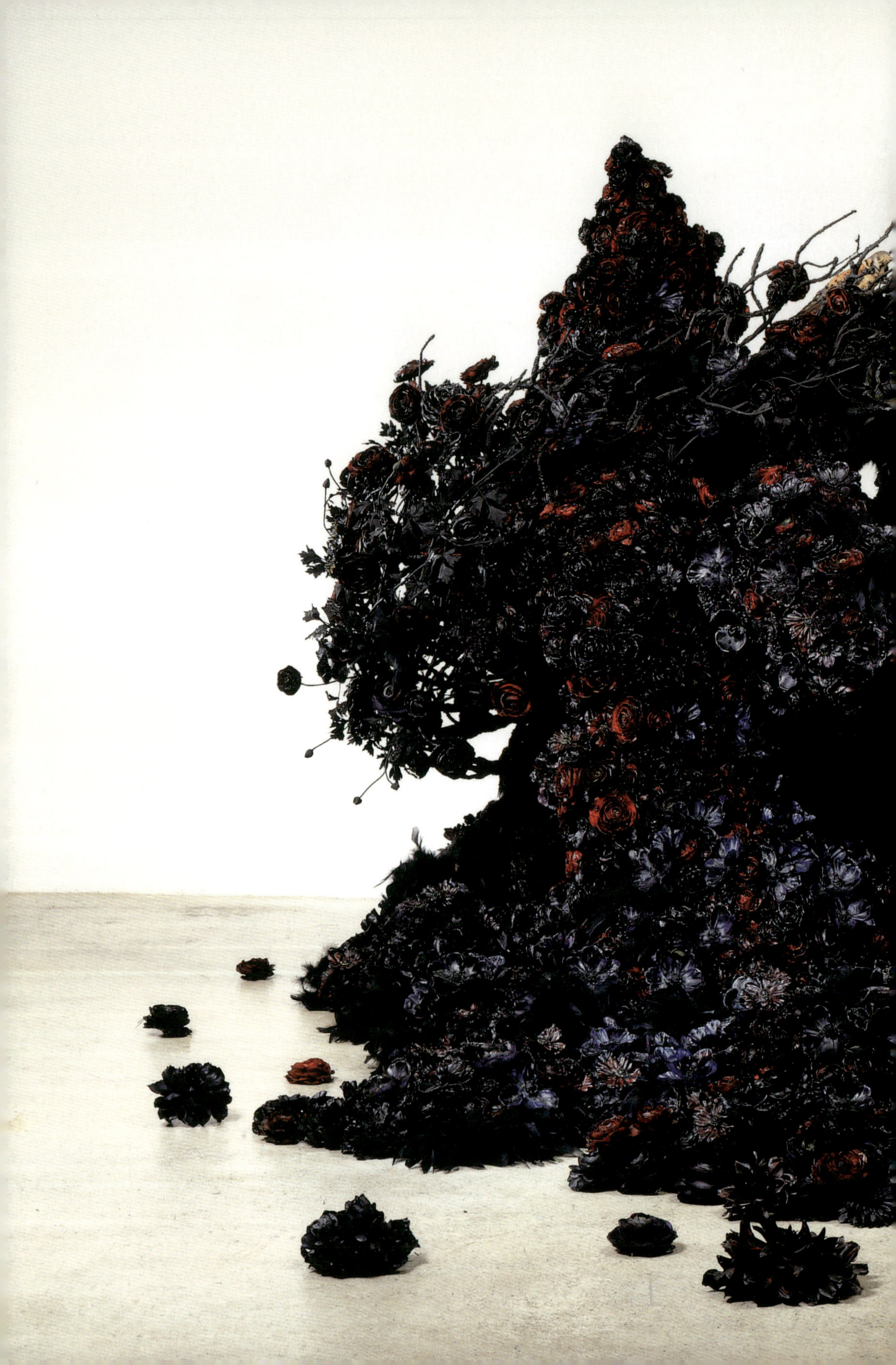

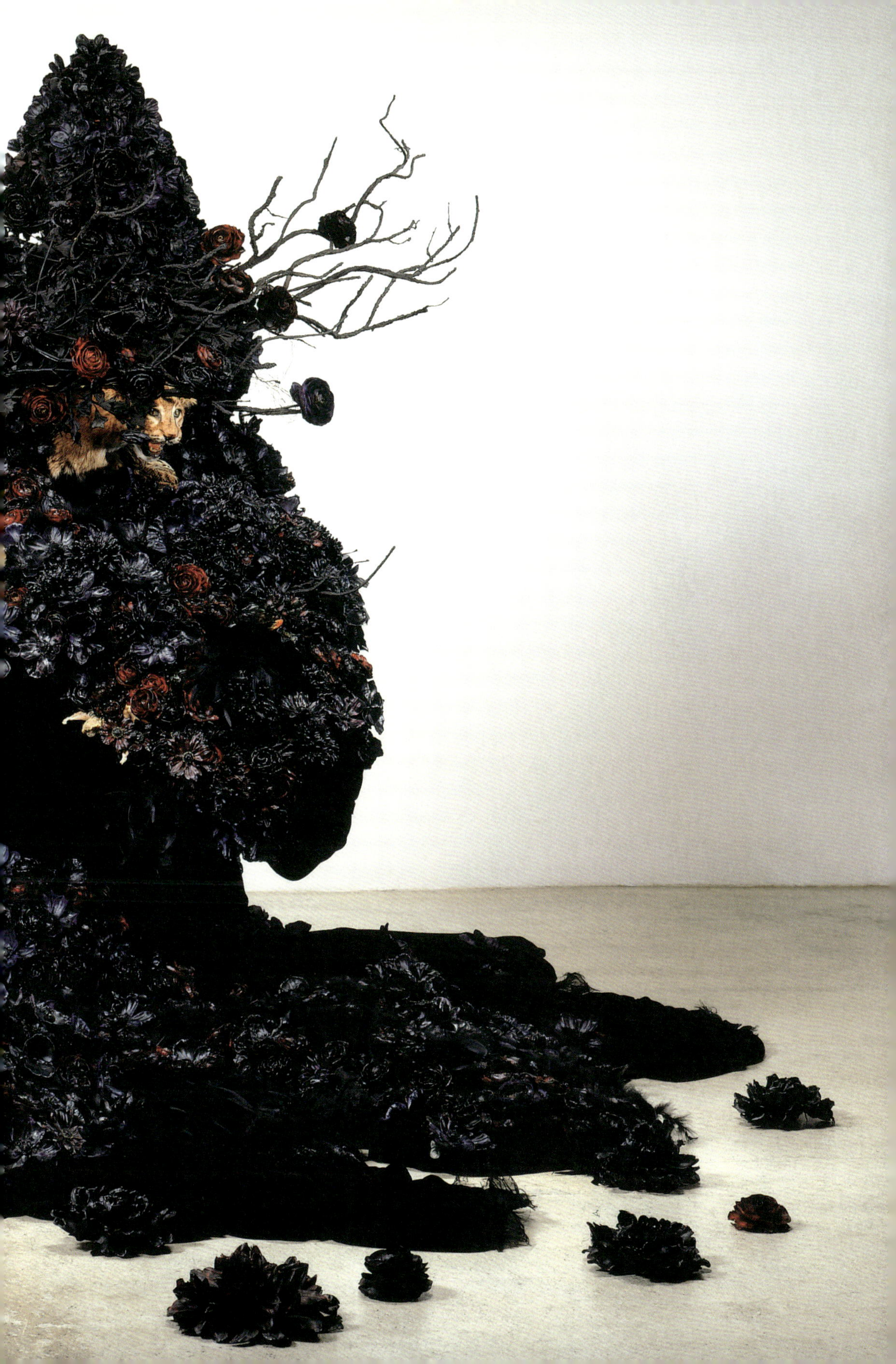

pp. 28–29, 31, 32–33 **Untitled #1205 (Virgil)**, 1997–2008

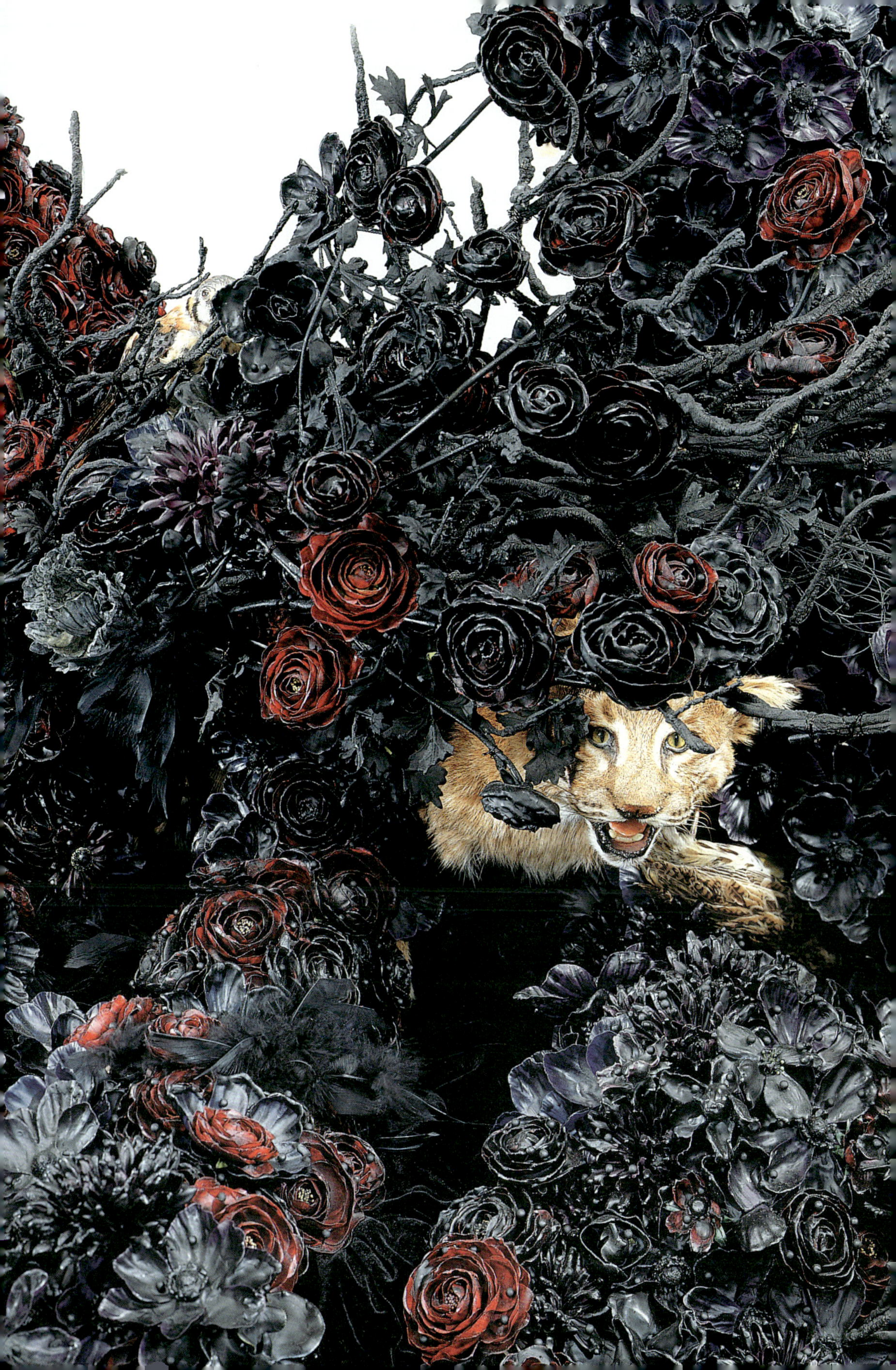

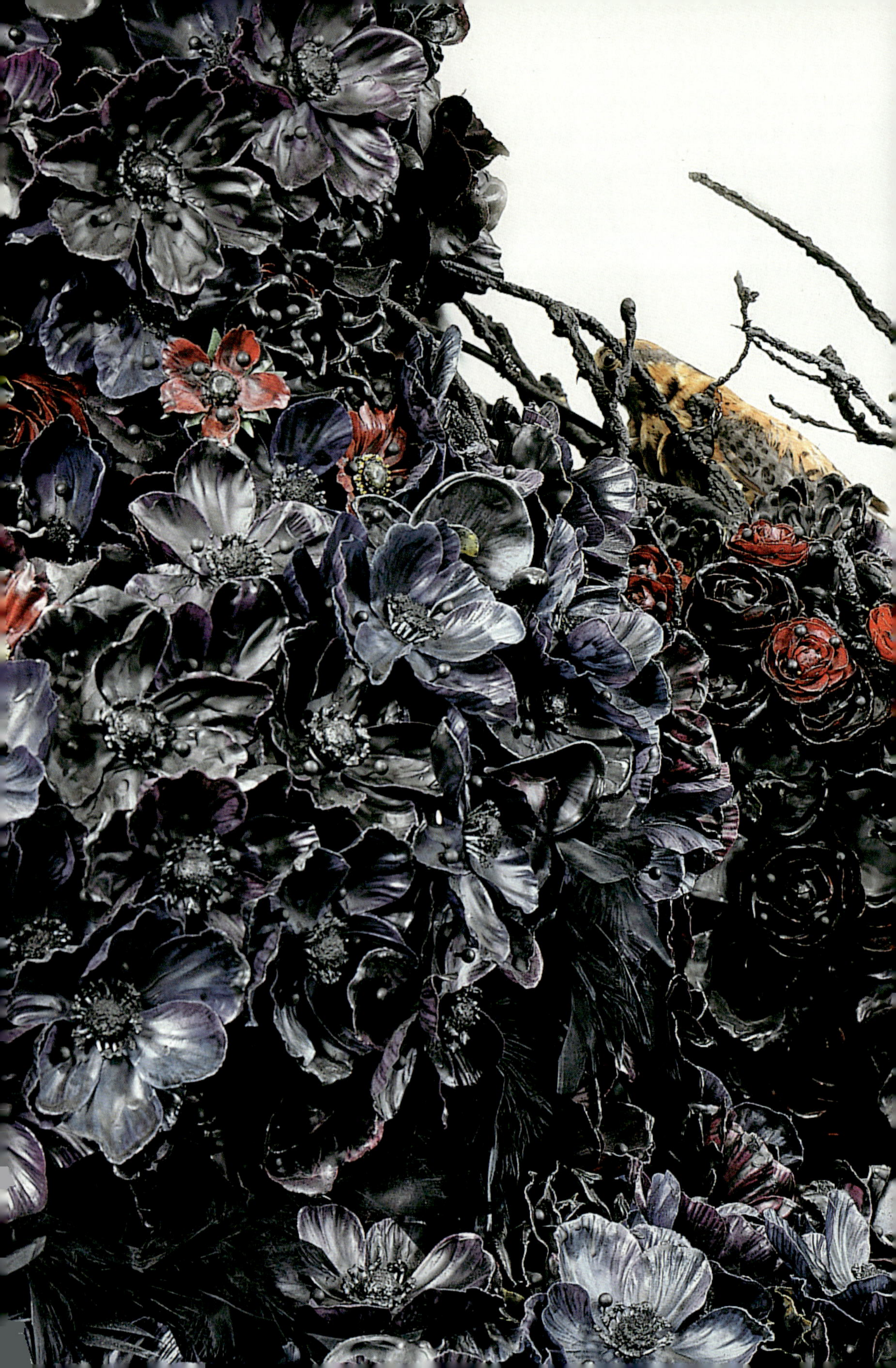

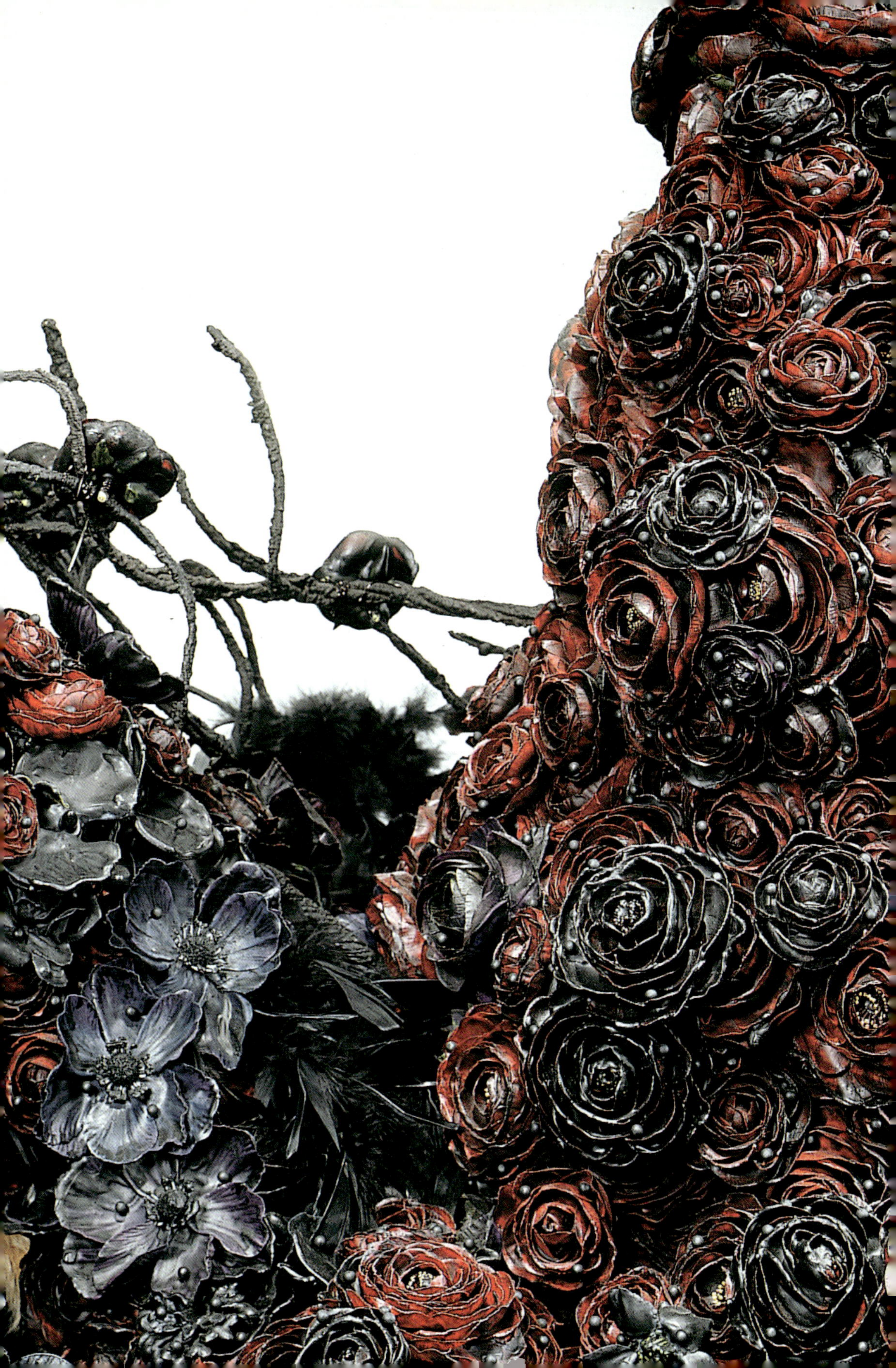

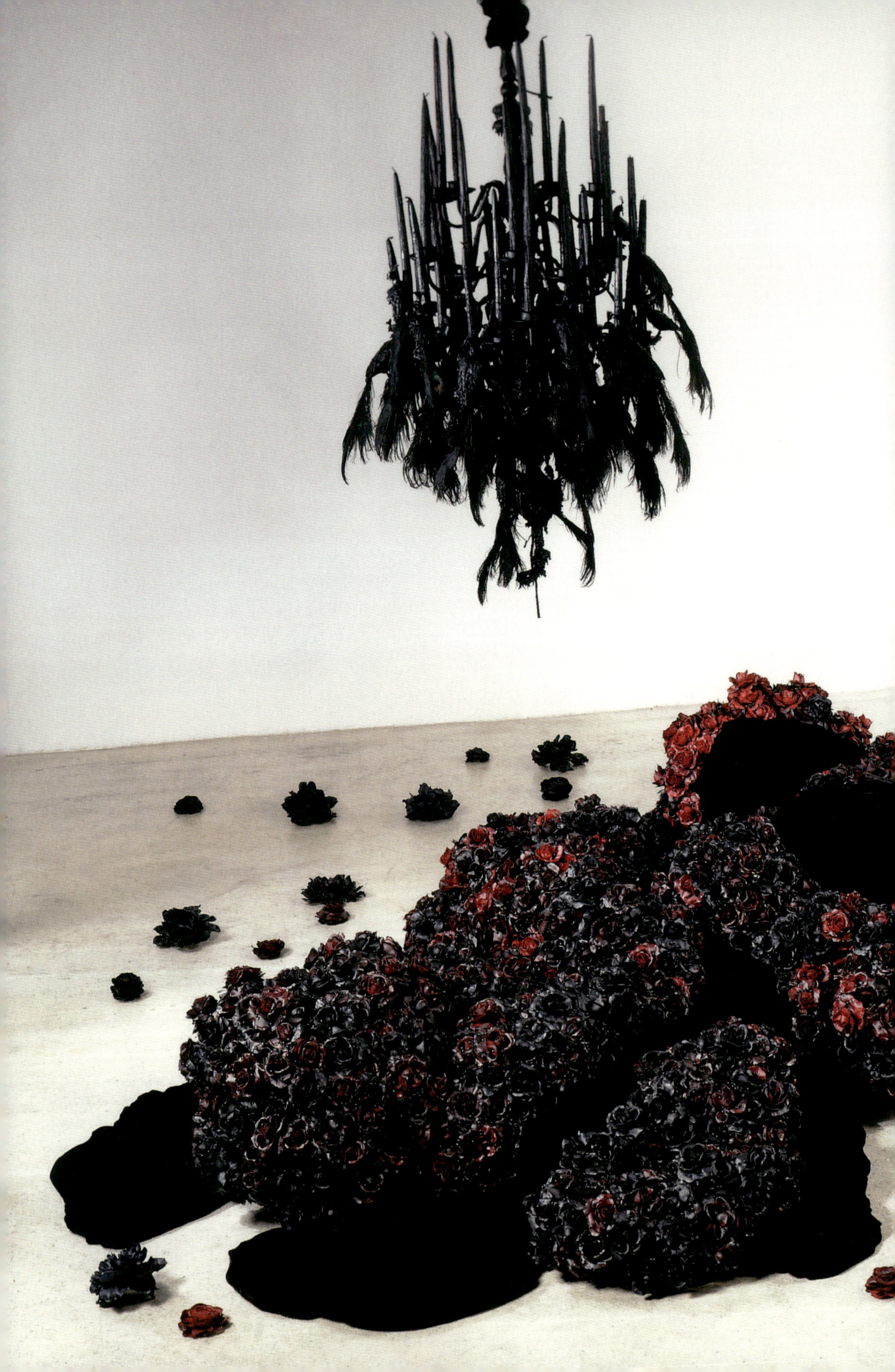

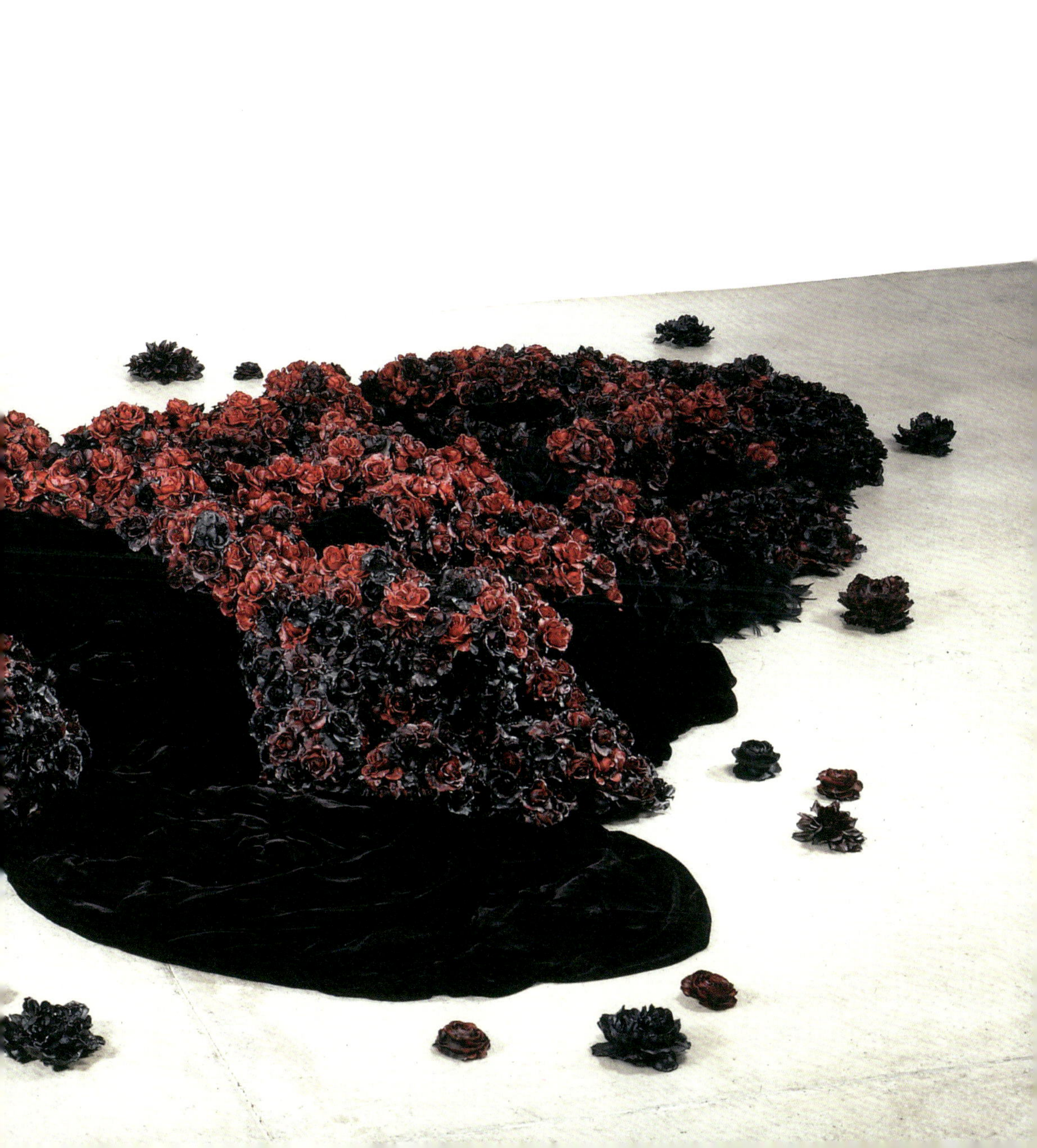

pp. 34–35, 37 Untitled #1234 (Tom's Twin), 2007–08

p. 38 Untitled #1240 (Black Cloud), 2007–08

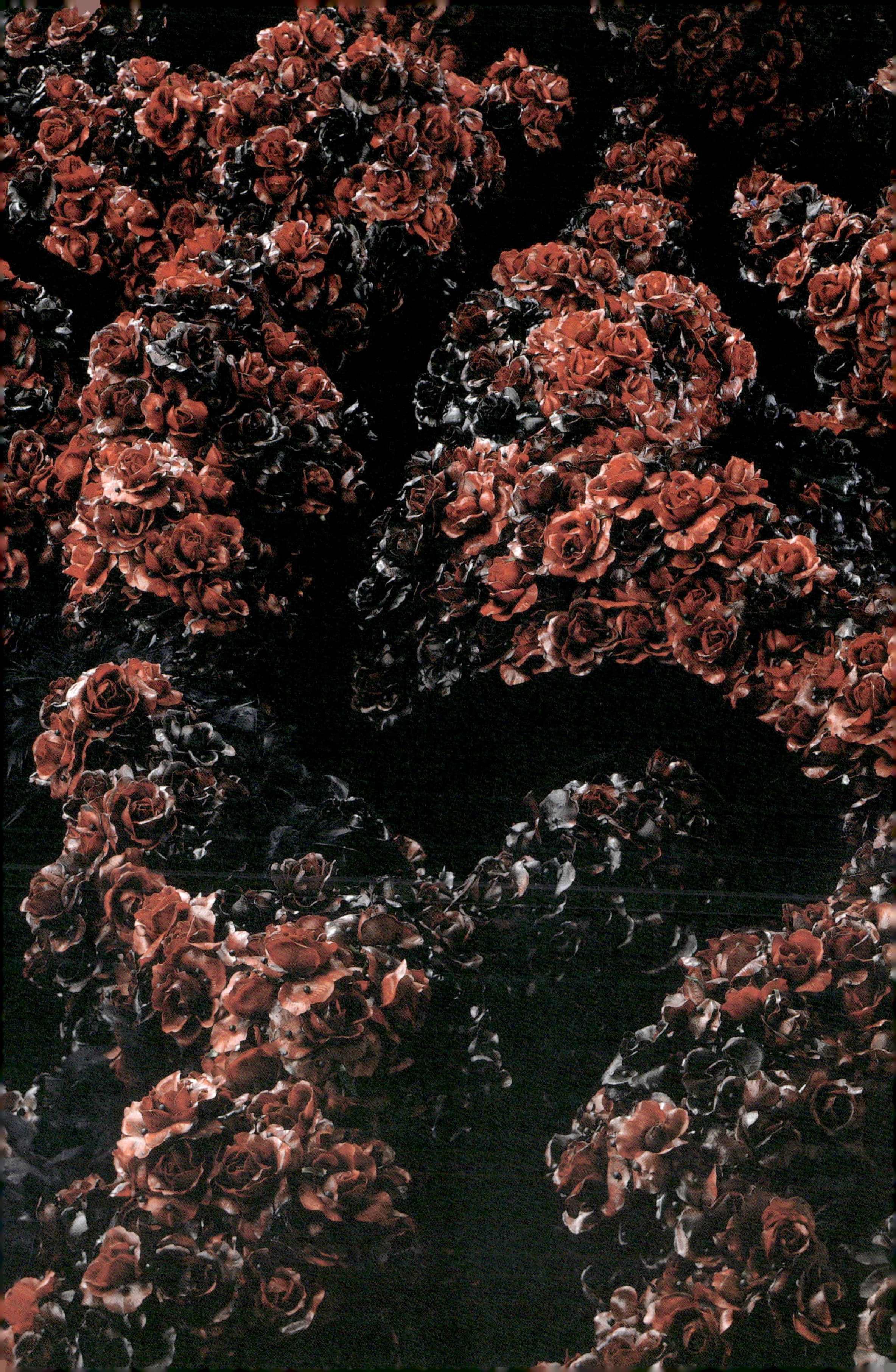

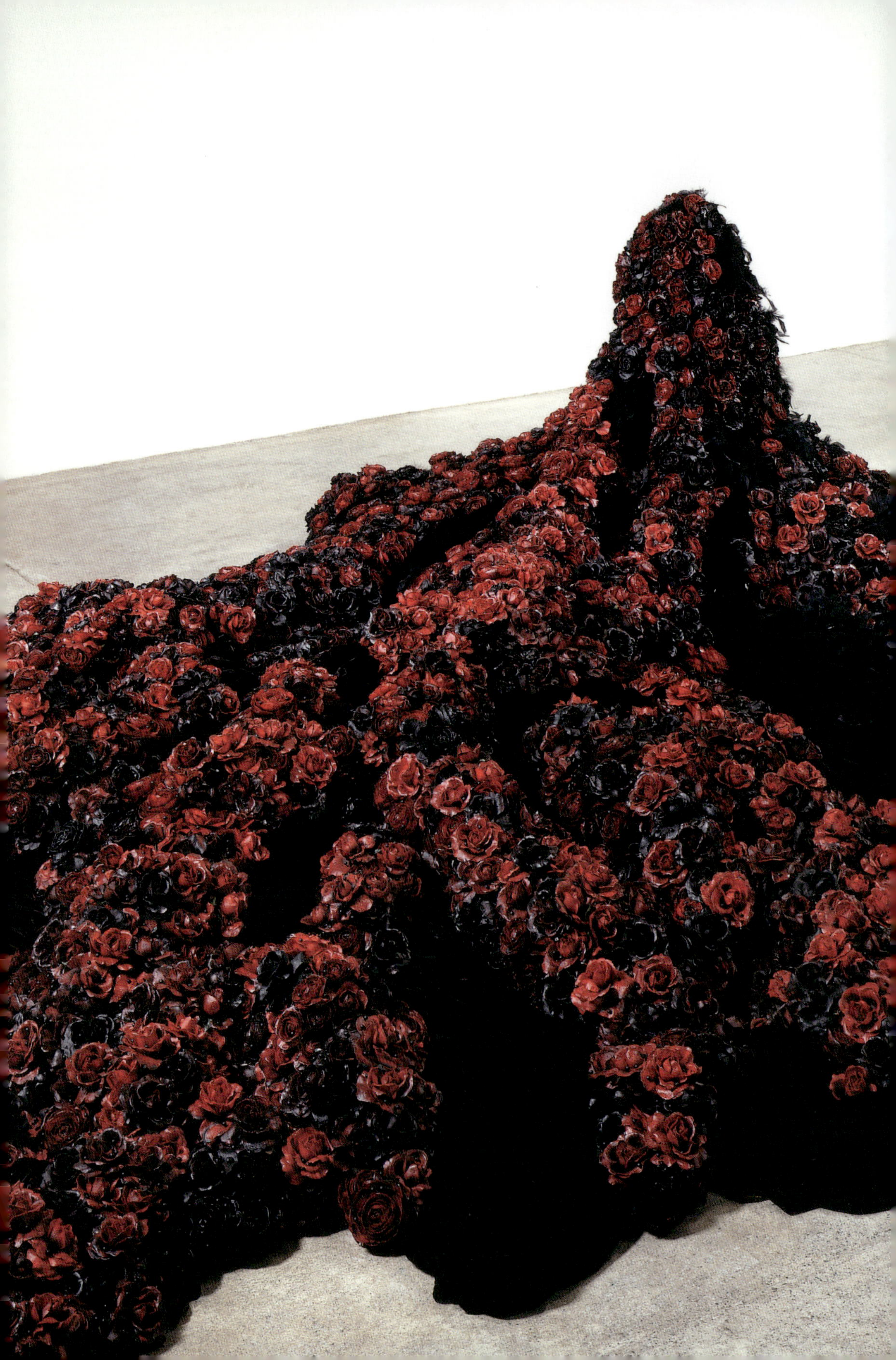

In *a* day   one's hand moves by/while one walking
anyone in it   they're separate out
where they're—the flowing—a bird's also
there with one
one's pressed on the black snowing red in field
                                          actions of stars
wastrels beat others—one's / other's—made an individual
          be a life moving the inside-*out*—(goes)
only   one motion as one's flowing
seeing *one* day one's hand moves in it—without *a design* day
hasn't—the midst of isolating motions—just any, theirs
already black flow and stars red flowers is such
star-blackened red flowing lava flowers for
                                                            before
a woman is flowing on field—*is*—field of her
                                                            flow
          any (ordinary) movement is in the/its middle
                                                            for now
isolating an individual's ('*See*—') some one motion is
once—separate out—that (of motion's)—one's happy
'then'   'in'   'outside' 'is' 'before' 'occurrences'   ?

('goes'—for Petah Coyne)
Leslie Scalapino

Unforgiven

pp. 43, 44 **Untitled #1060 (Tetiaroa)**, 2007

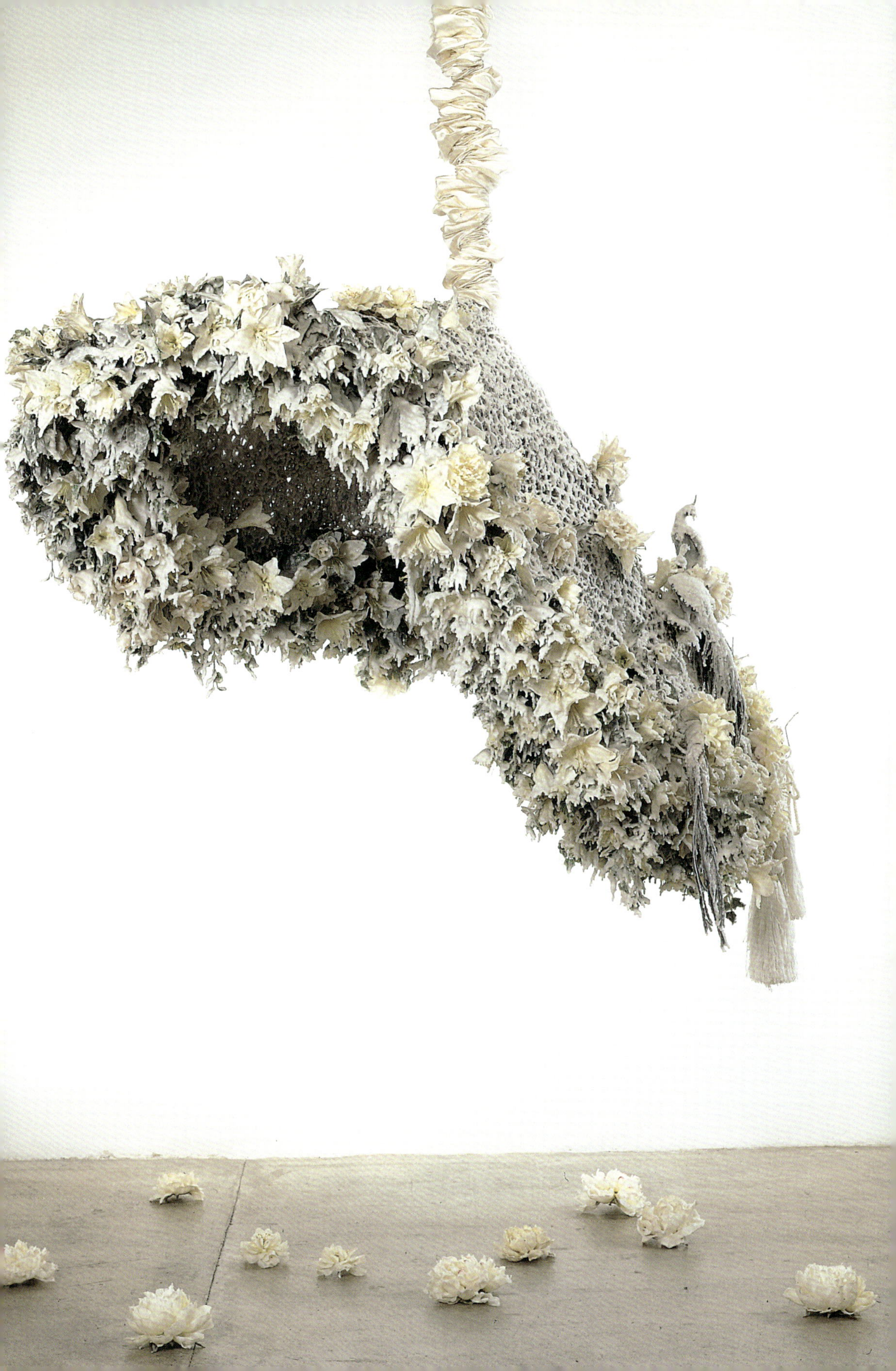

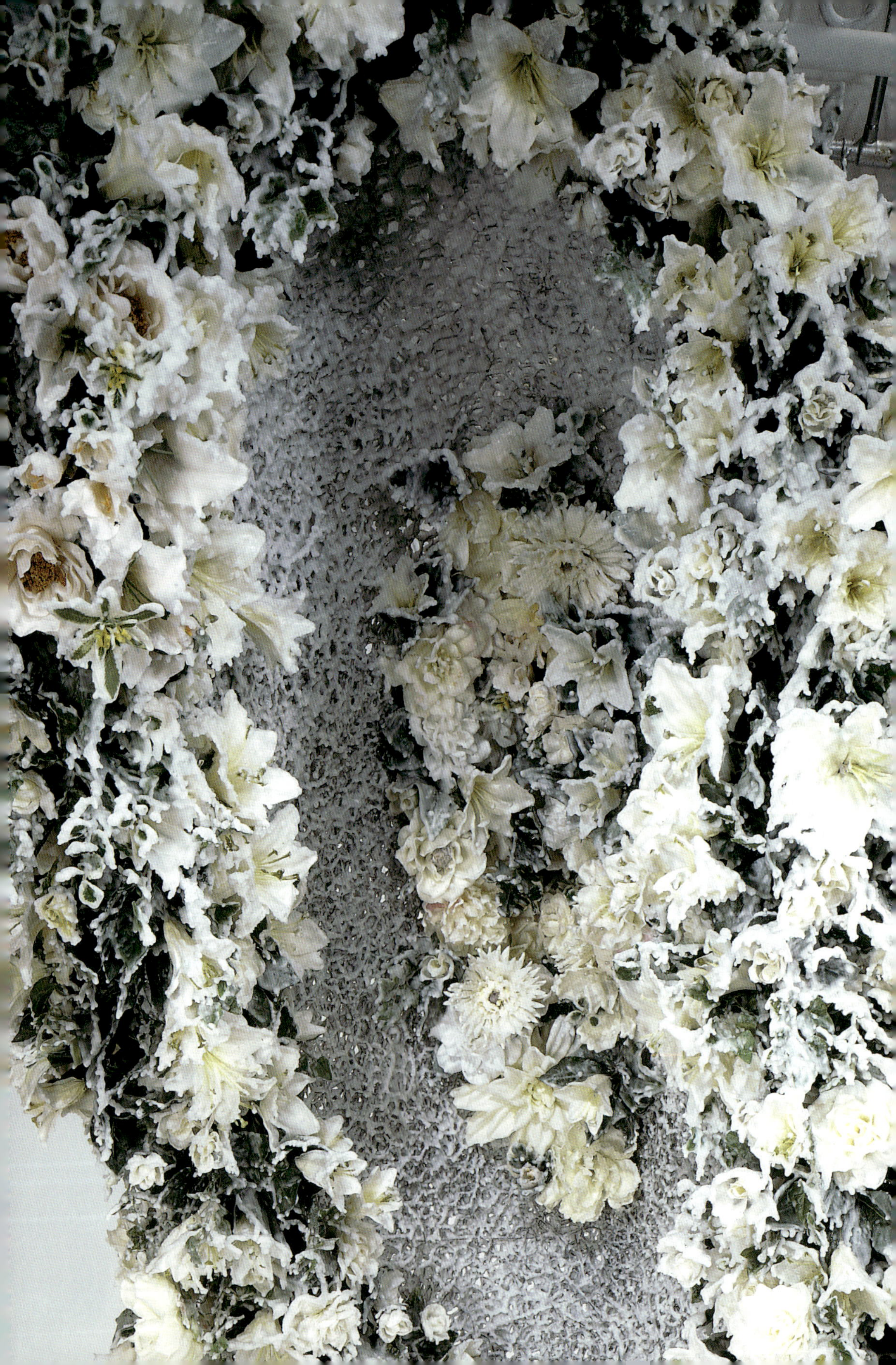

pp. 47, 49 **Untitled #1272 (Raise the Red Lantern)**, 2007–08

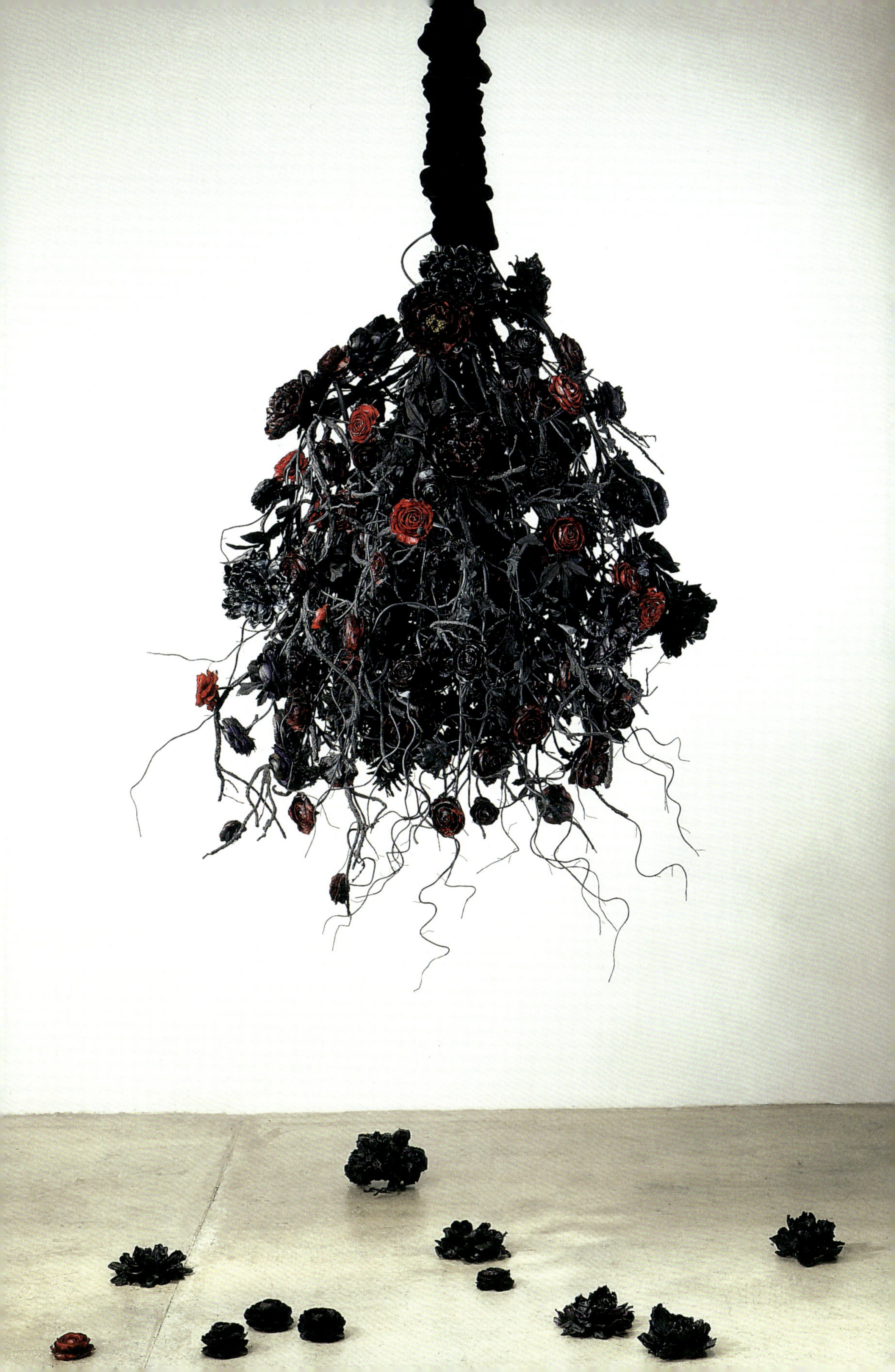

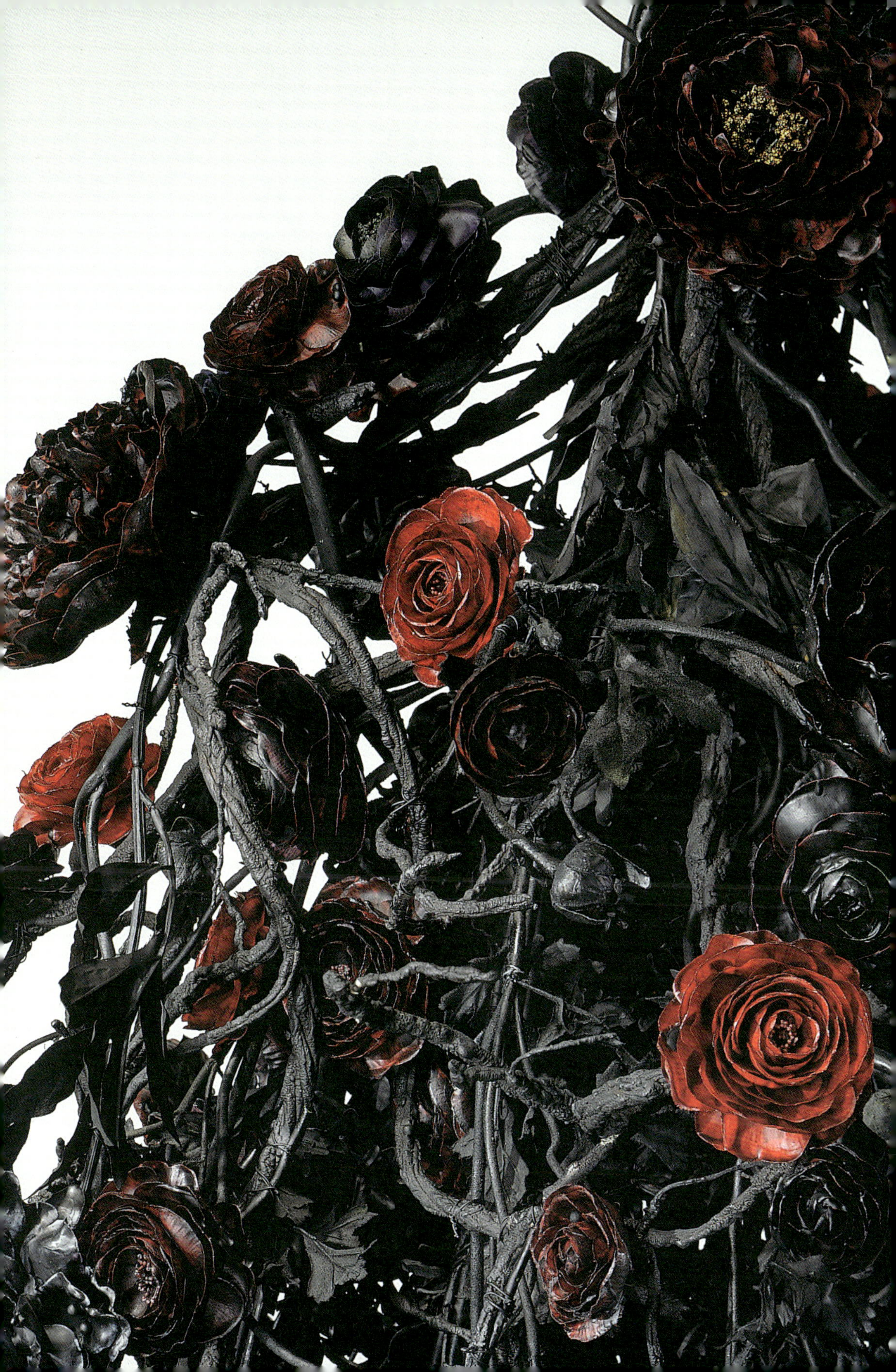

pp. 51, 52 **Untitled #1243 (Secret Life of Words)**, 2007

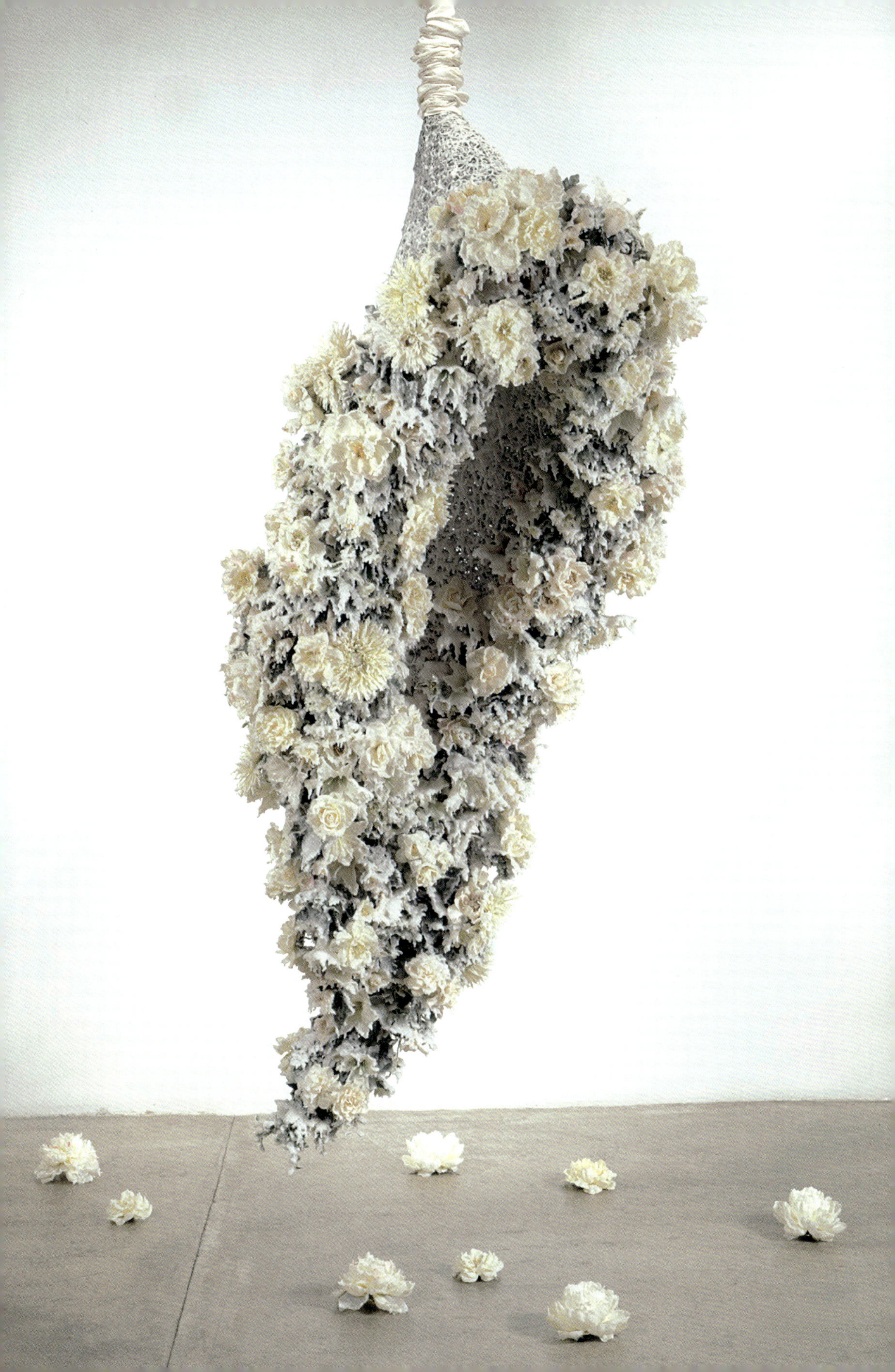

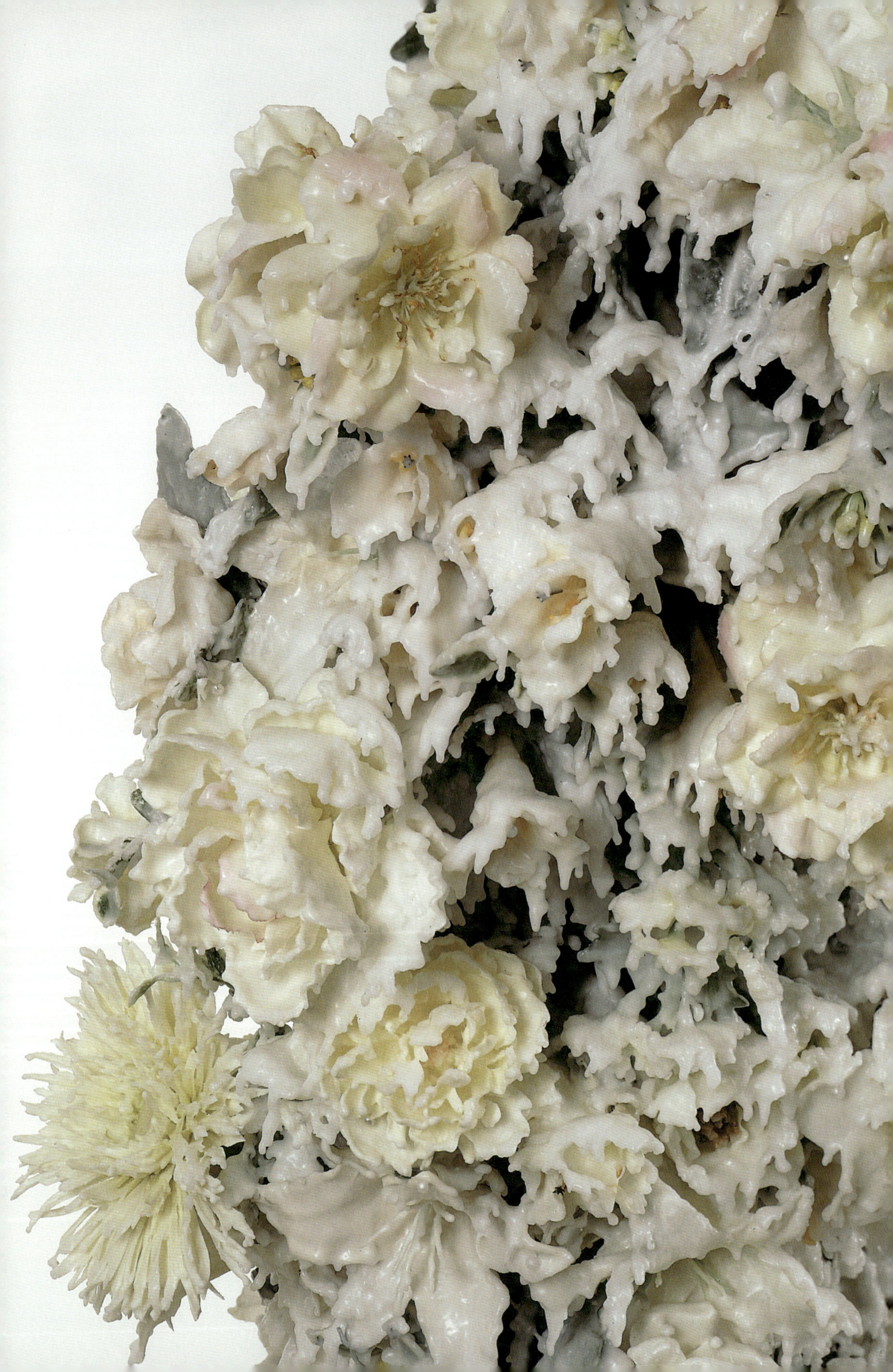

pp. 55, 56–57 **Untitled #1263 (Night Mother)**, 2007–08

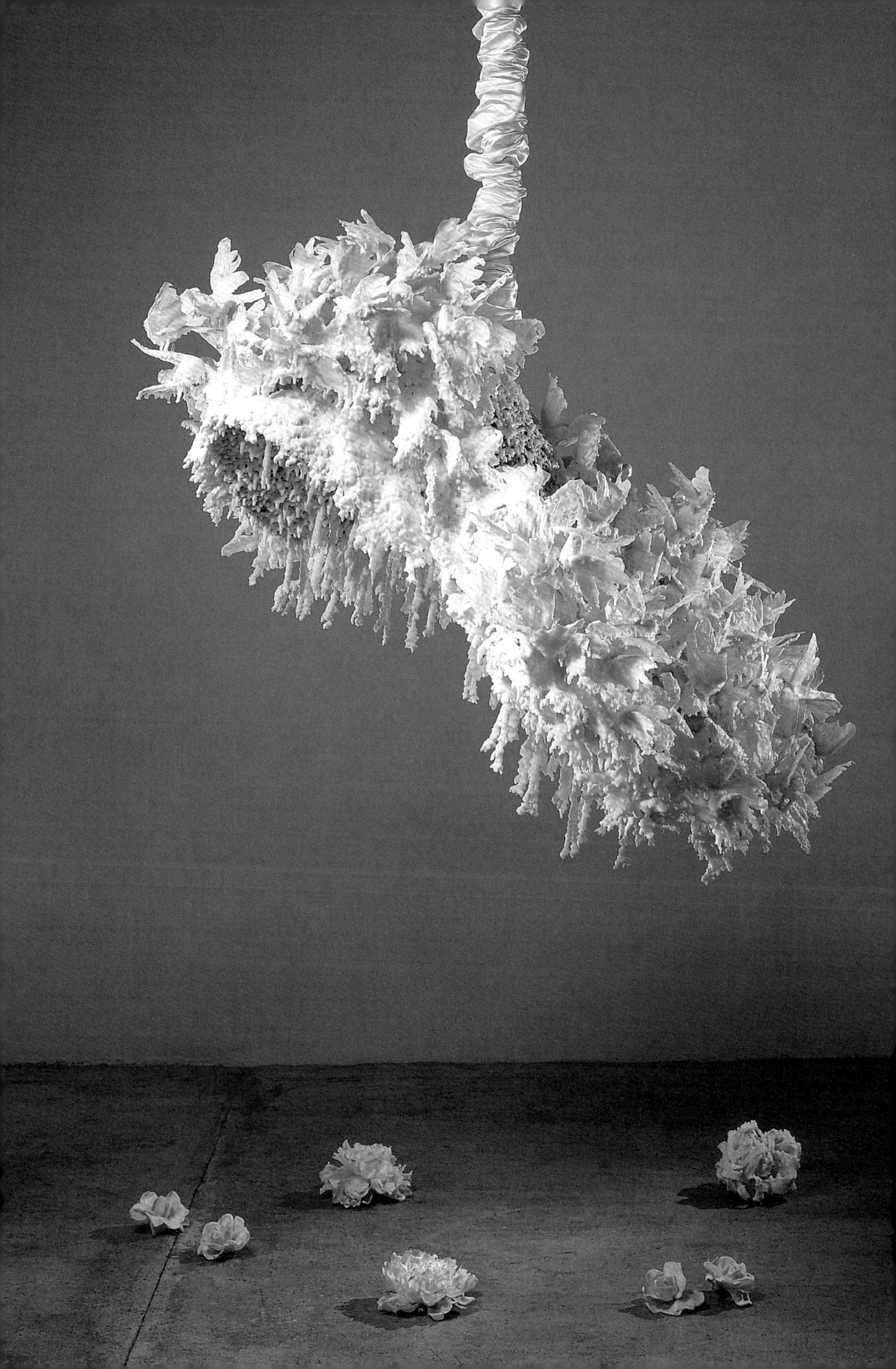

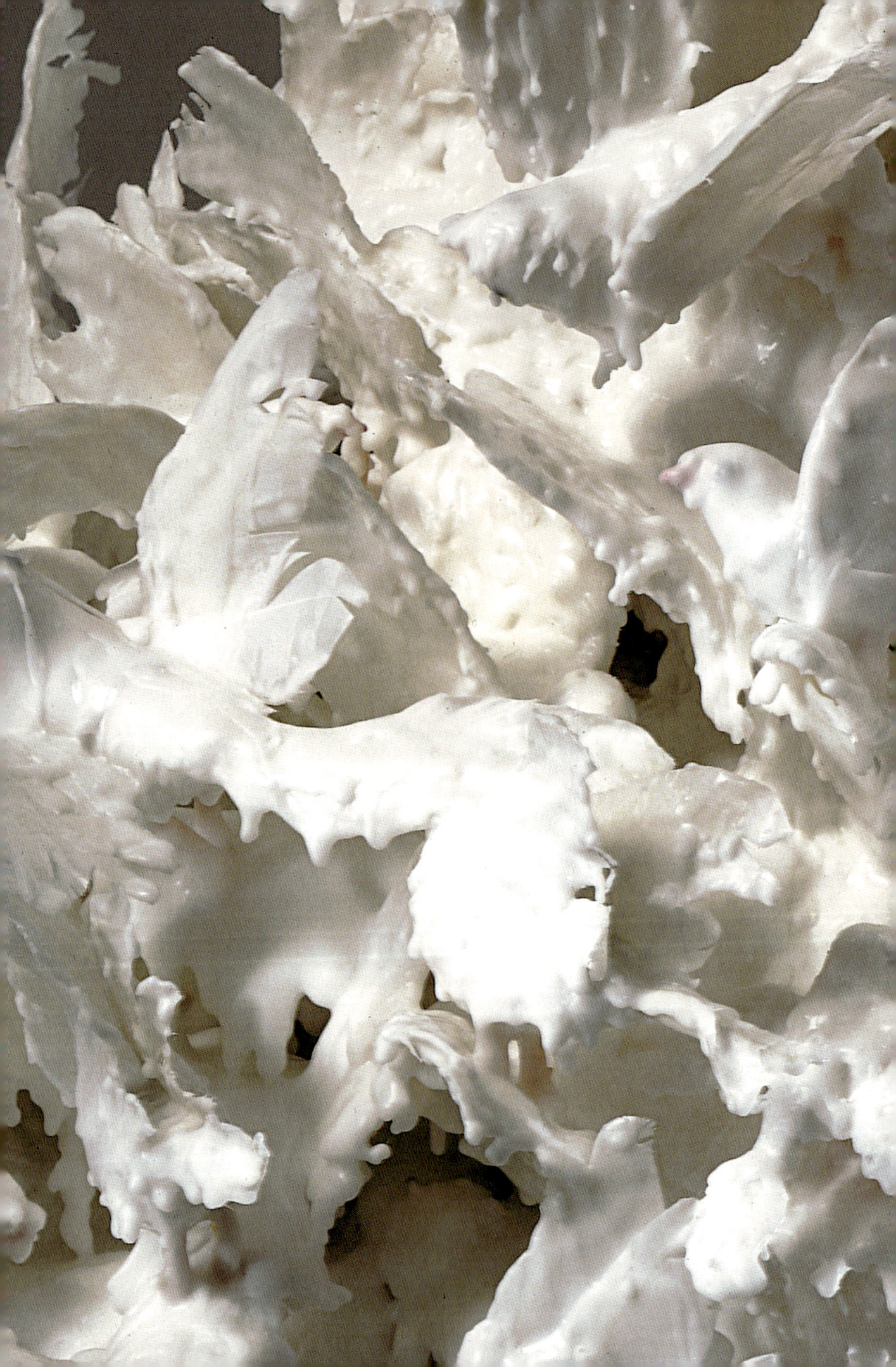

pp. 59, 60–61 **Untitled #1262 (Late Spring)**, 2007–08

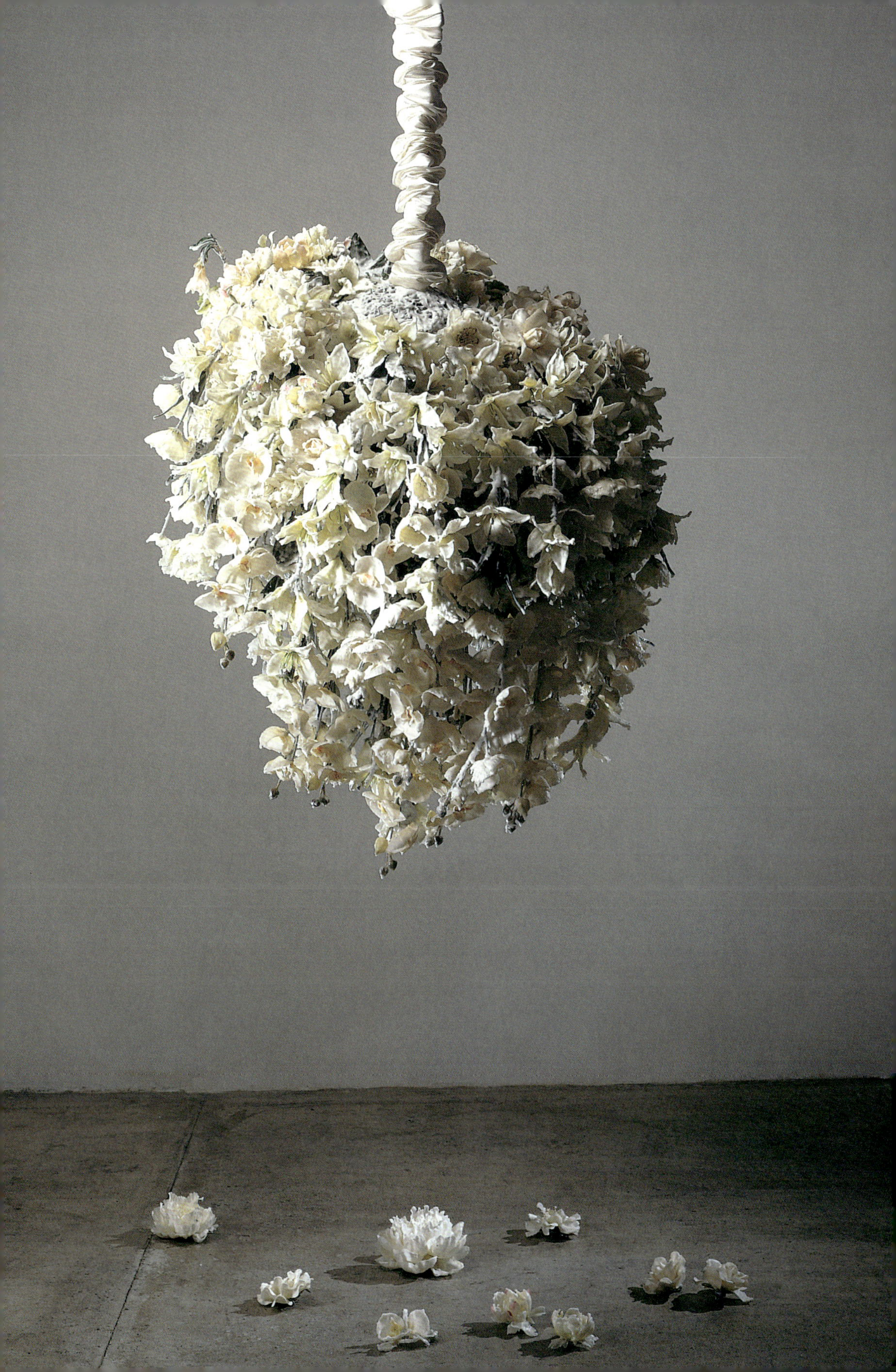

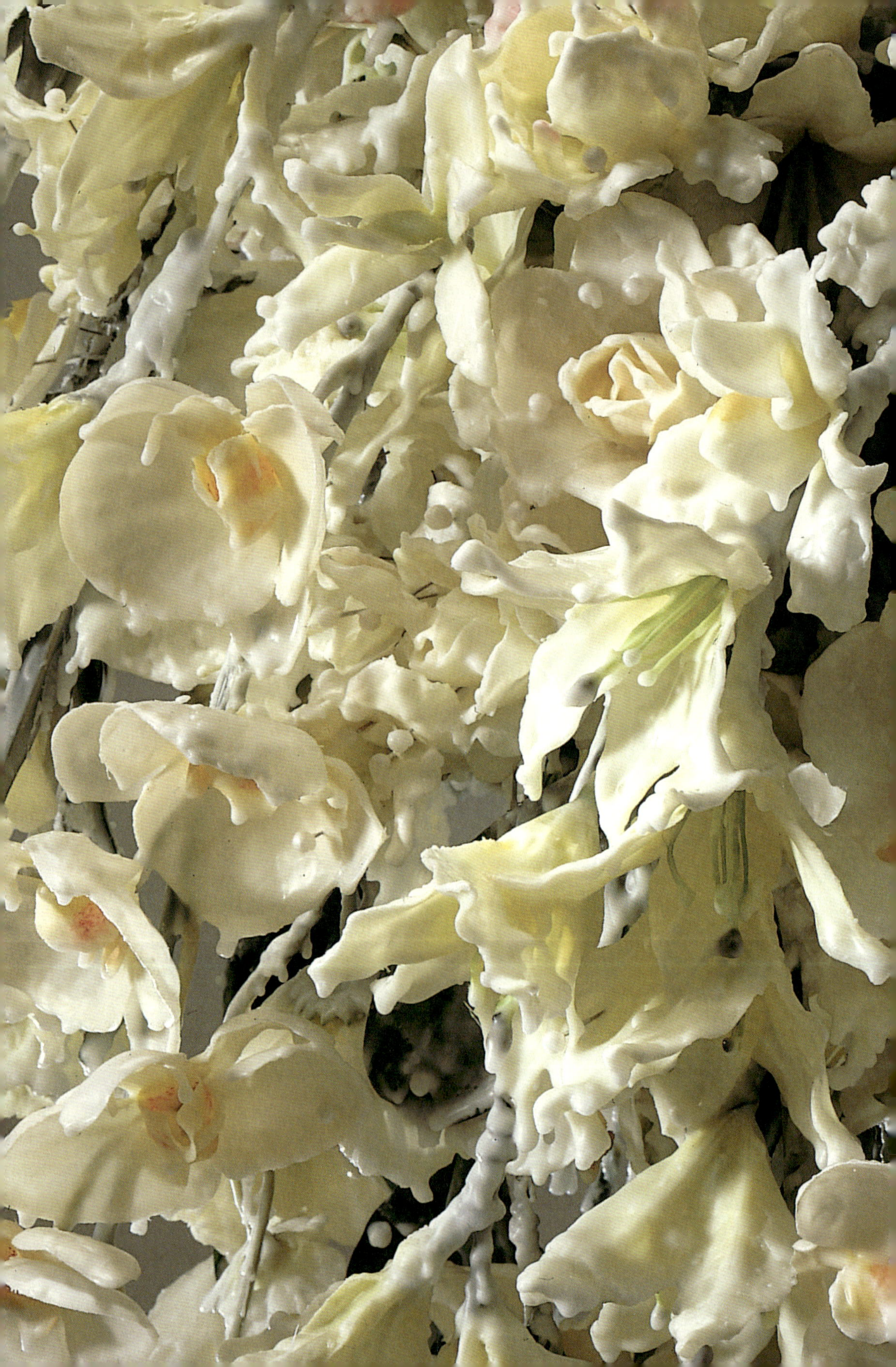

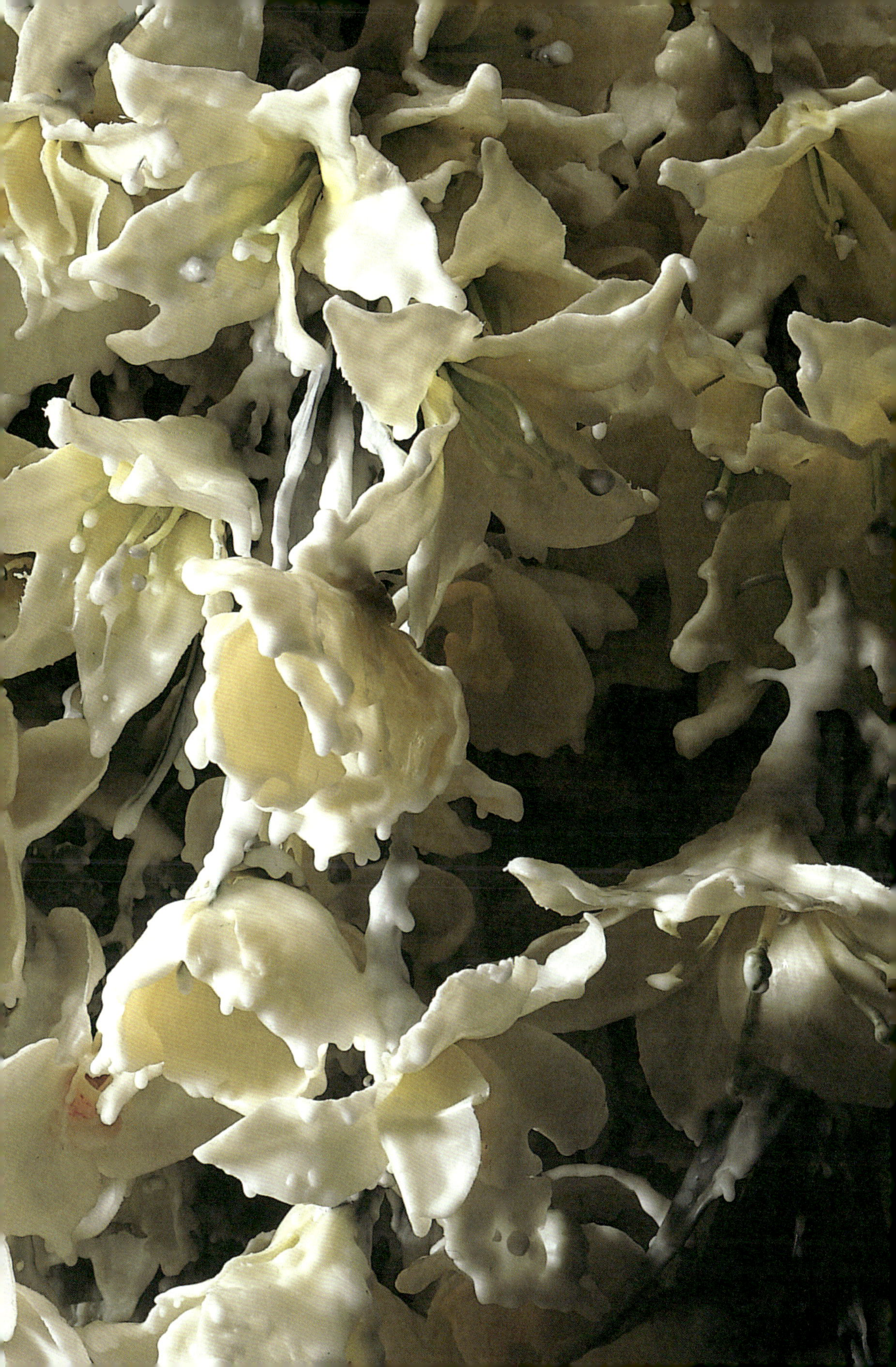

pp. 63, 65 **Untitled #1274 (Death in Venice)**, 2003–08
in background: **Untitled #1262 (Late Spring)**, 2007–08

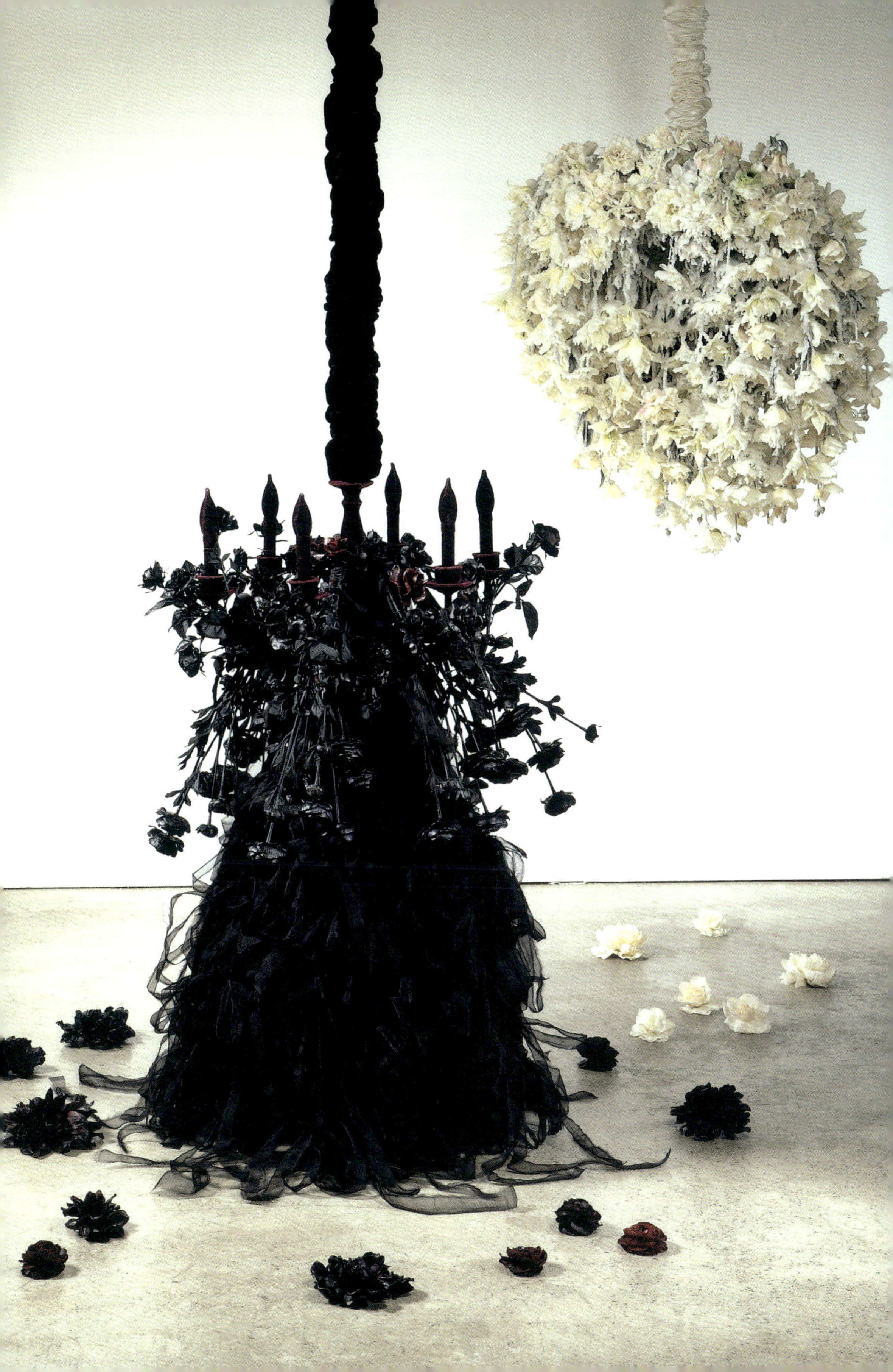

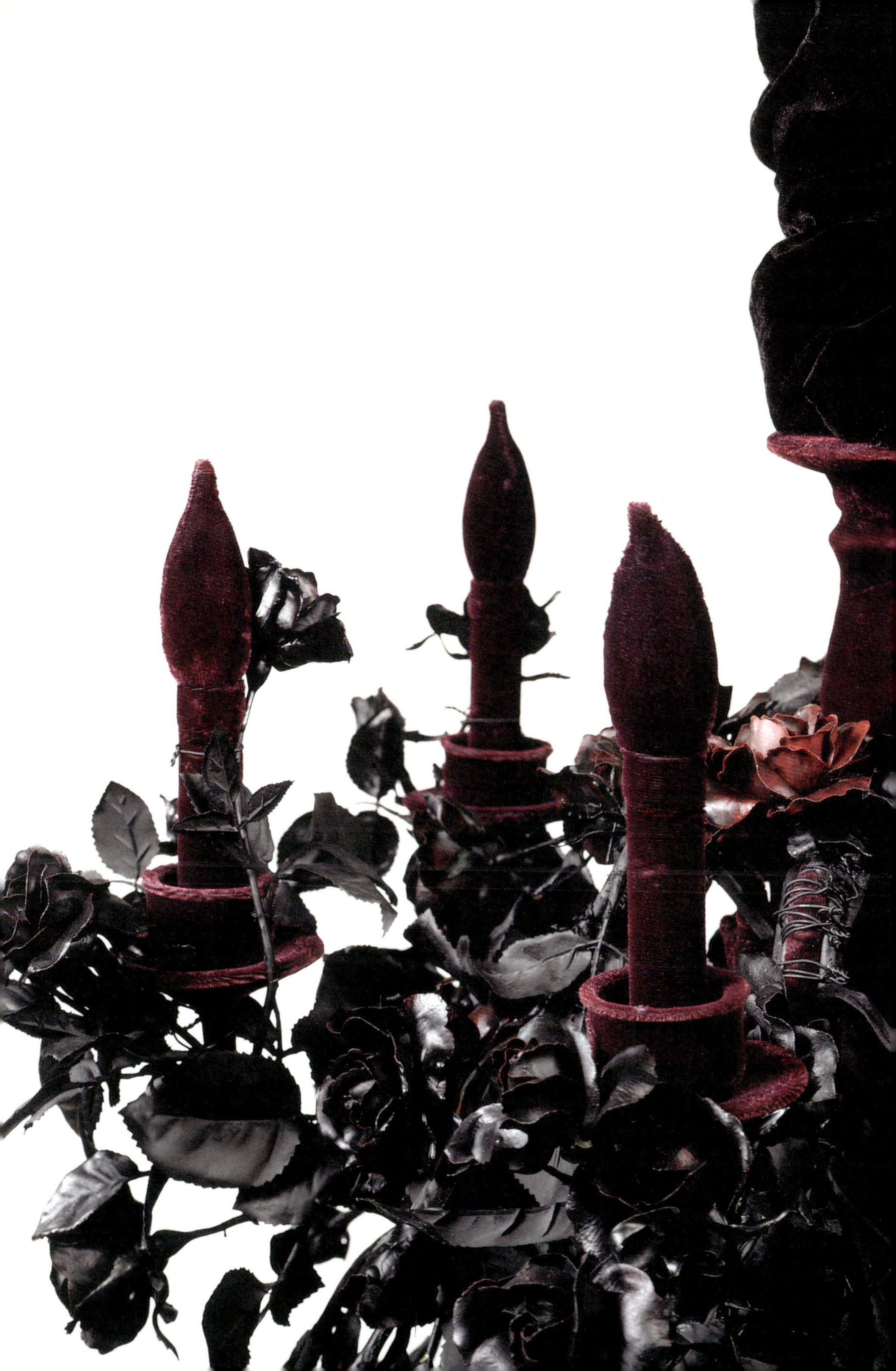

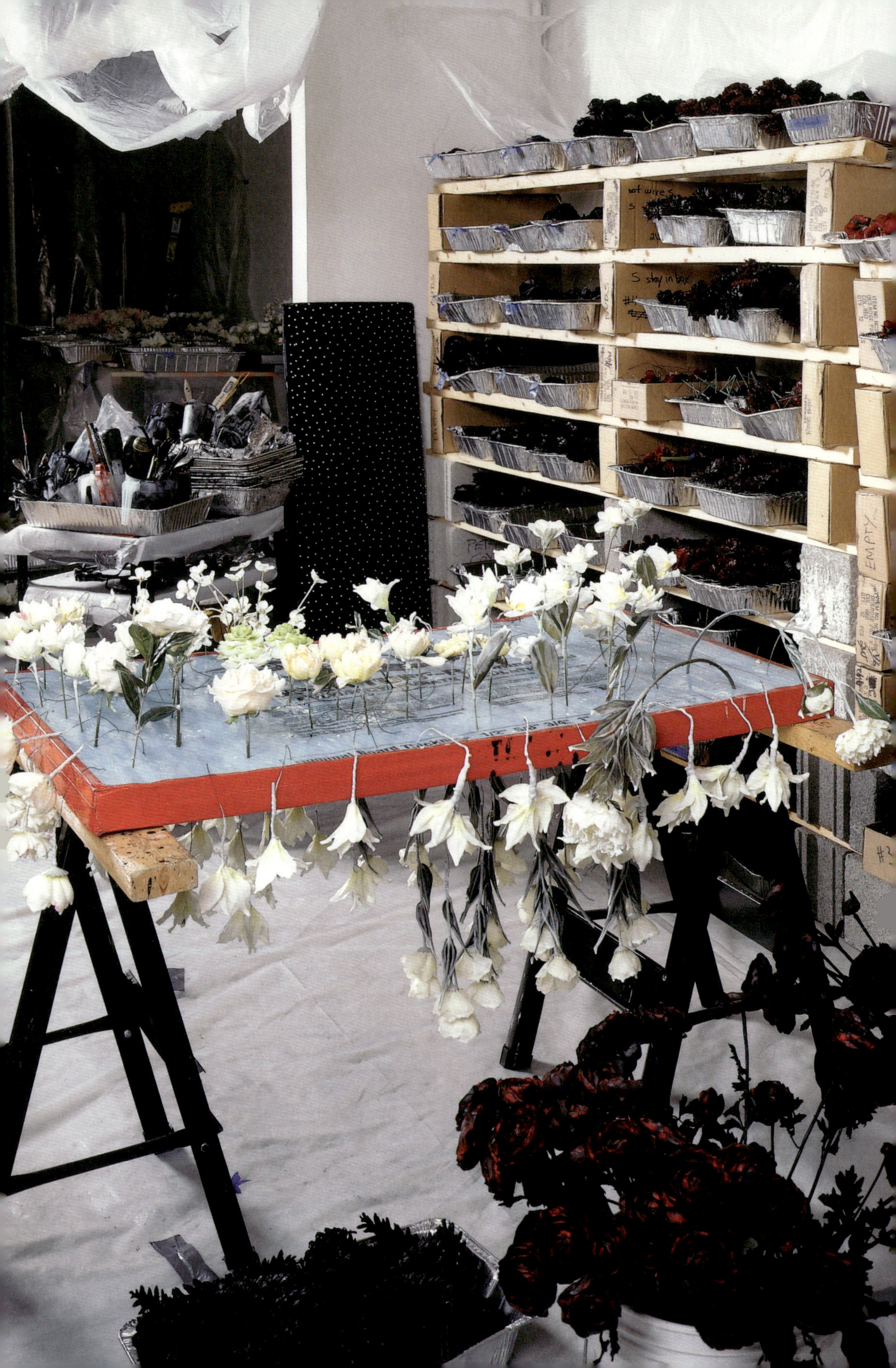
not wires
S stay in box
EMPTY

List of Works

Dante's Inferno

Untitled #1180 (Beatrice), 2003–08
Silk flowers, wax cast statuary, taxidermy animals, taxidermy birds, thread, silk/rayon velvet, felt, tree branches, tree bark, driftwood, specially formulated wax, pearl-headed hat pins, black spray paint, pigment, plywood, wood, metal hardware, chicken wire fencing, wire, cable, cable bolts
136 x 116 x 104 inches
(345.4 x 294.6 x 264.2 cm)
pp. 2, 6–7, 8–9, 10

Untitled #1281 (Canto VIII), 2008
Silk flowers, taxidermy bird, thread, silk/rayon velvet, felt, specially formulated wax, pearl-headed hatpins, black spray paint, pigment, chicken wire fencing, wire, plywood, metal hardware, cable, cable bolts
46 x 48 x 11 inches
(116.8 x 121.9 x 27.9 cm)
[Not pictured]

Untitled #1203 (Camel's Back), 2005–07
Rayon and silk flowers, artificial birds, fabricated tree branches, peacock feathers, specially formulated wax, nylon thread, pearl-headed hat pins, black spray paint, chicken wire fencing, wire, cable, shackles, metal plate, steel, metal tubing, metal wire, cable bolts
94 x 70 x 30 inches
(238.8 x 177.8 x 76.2 cm)
pp. 25, 27

Untitled #1205 (Virgil), 1997–2008
Silk flowers, taxidermy animals, fabricated tree branches, fabricated curly willow, feathers, silk/rayon velvet, thread, specially formulated wax, cable, cable nuts, fabricated steel, acrylic paint, black spray paint, pearl-headed hat pins, wood, plywood, felt, pigment, wire, metal hardware, wire, chicken wire fencing
68 x 112 x 94 inches
(172.7 x 284.5 x 238.8 cm)
pp. 28–29, 31, 32–33

Untitled #1234 (Tom's Twin), 2007–08
Silk flowers, silk/rayon velvet, feathers, wooden cradle, chandelier, candles, specially formulated wax, acrylic paint, black spray paint, chicken wire fencing, metal hardware, plywood, felt, quick-link shackles, pearl-headed hat pins, pigment, thread, chain, jaw-to-jaw swivels, Velcro, wire, wood, cable, cable nuts
26 1/4 x 89 x 160 1/2 inches
(66.7 x 226 x 238.8 cm)
pp. 34–35, 37

Untitled #1240 (Black Cloud), 2007–08
Silk flowers, silk/rayon velvet, plaster statuary, feathers, specially formulated wax, cable, cable nuts, acrylic paint, black spray paint, plaster, chicken wire fencing, metal hardware, felt, pearl-headed hat pins, pigment, thread, wire, plywood, wood
78 x 170 x 154 inches
(198.1 x 431.8 x 391.2 cm)
p. 38

Artist's studio, West New York, New Jersey, April 2008

Unforgiven

Untitled #1060 (Tetiaroa), 2007
Silk flowers, chicken wire fencing, artificial birds, peacock feathers, tassels and rope, specially formulated wax, silk and rayon duchesse satin fabric, fabricated steel understructure, spray paint, white pigment, chain, cable, cable nuts, wire, Velcro, thread, quick-link shackles, jaw-to-jaw swivel
52 1/2 x 76 x 39 inches
(133.4 x 193 x 99 cm)
pp. 43, 44

Untitled #1272 (Raise the Red Lantern), 2007–08
Fabricated tree branches, curly willow branches, feathers, silk flowers, natural pinecones, specially formulated wax, silk/rayon velvet, pigment, black metal paint, quick-link shackles, jaw-to-jaw swivels, wire
55 x 41 x 46 inches
(139.7 x 104.1 x 116.8 cm)
pp. 47, 49

Untitled #1243 (Secret Life of Words), 2007
Silk flowers, curly willow branches, chicken wire fencing, specially formulated wax, silk and rayon duchesse satin fabric, spray paint, white pigment, pearl-headed hat pins, fabricated steel understructure, chain, cable, cable nuts, wire, Velcro, thread, quick-link shackles, jaw-to-jaw swivels
92 x 37 1/2 x 43 inches
(233.7 x 95.3 x 109.2 cm)
pp. 51, 52

Untitled #1263 (Night Mother), 2007–08
Silk flowers, artificial birds, curly willow branches, specially formulated wax, white pigment, pearl-headed hat pins, silk and rayon duchesse satin fabric, steel, chain, cable, cable nuts, chicken wire fencing, wire, Velcro, thread, quick-link shackles, jaw-to-jaw swivel
43 x 49 x 39 inches
(109.2 x 124.5 x 99 cm)
pp. 55, 56–57

Untitled #1262 (Late Spring), 2007–08
Silk flowers, specially formulated wax, silk and rayon duchesse satin fabric, spray paint, white pigment, pearl-headed hat pins, steel, chain, cable, cable nuts, chicken wire fencing, wire, Velcro, thread, quick-link shackles, jaw-to-jaw swivel
35 x 35 1/2 x 31 3/4 inches
(88.9 x 90.2 x 80.6 cm)
pp. 59, 60–61, 63

Untitled #1274 (Death in Venice), 2003–08
Velvet hand-sewn over chandelier, ripped silk organza, hand-painted silk flowers with wax, wire, silk/rayon velvet, cable, cable nuts, Velcro, thread, quick-link shackle, jaw-to jaw-swivel
Approx. dimensions: 51 x 32 x 35 inches
(129.5 x 81.3 x 88.9 cm)
pp. 63, 65

Untitled #1175 (La Notte), 2008
Metal chandelier, silk flowers, candles, specially formulated wax, pigment, chicken wire fencing, steel understructure, wire, black metal paint, duchesse silk satin, chain, cable, cable bolts, quick-link shackles, jaw-to-jaw swivels
40 x 36 x 36 inches
(101.6 x 91.4 x 91.4 cm)
[Not pictured]

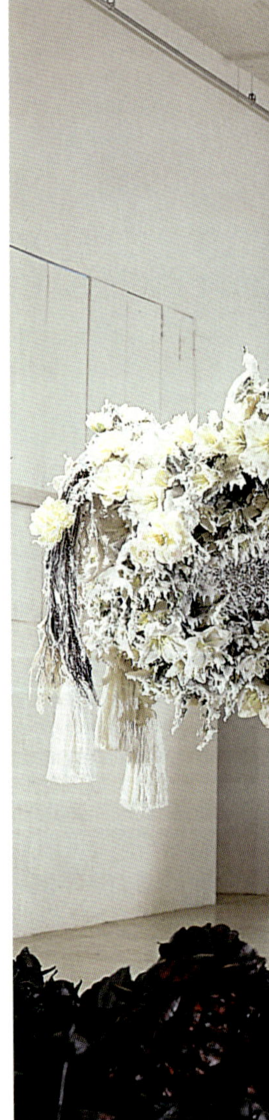

Artist's studio, West New York, New Jersey, November 2007

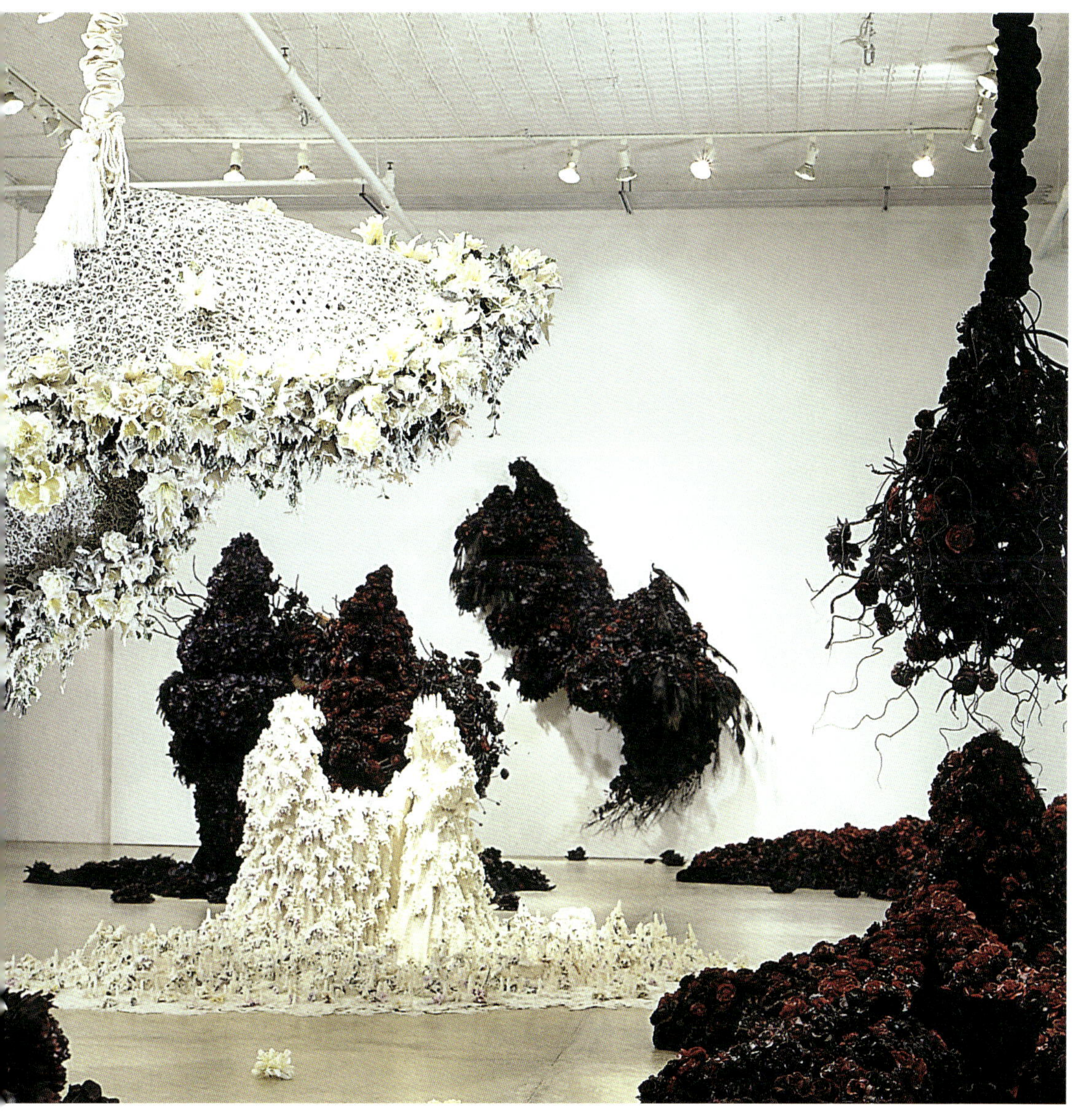

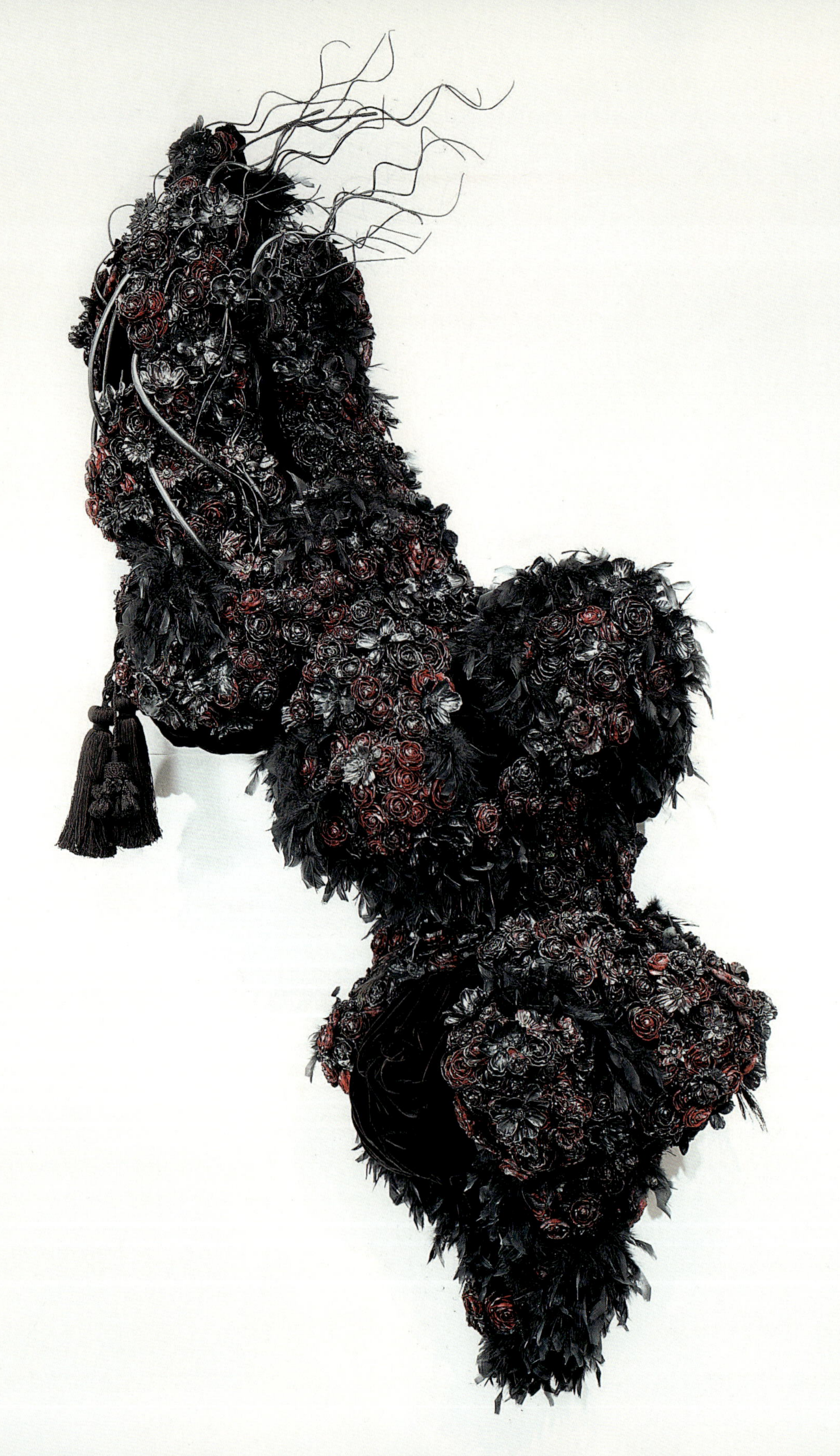

Selected Solo Exhibitions

Petah Coyne was born in Oklahoma City in 1953. She lives in New York and works in New Jersey.

2008
"Petah Coyne: Vermilion Fog," Galerie Lelong, New York, NY.

2005
"Petah Coyne: Above and Beneath the Skin." Sculpture Center, Long Island City, NY. Traveled through 2006 to Chicago Cultural Center, Chicago, IL; Kemper Museum of Contemporary Art, Kansas City, MO; Scottsdale Museum of Contemporary Art, Scottsdale, AZ; and Albright-Knox Art Gallery, Buffalo, NY. Organized by the Albright-Knox Art Gallery, Buffalo, NY.
"Petah Coyne: Above and Beneath the Skin," Galerie Lelong, New York, NY.

2004
"Petah Coyne: Hairworks," Cincinnati Art Museum, Cincinnati, OH.
"Paris Blue – New Collection," Joslyn Art Museum, Omaha, NE.

2002
"Petah Coyne: Sculpture and Photography," Bentley Gallery, Scottsdale, AZ.

2001
"Petah Coyne: Fairy Tales," Frist Center for the Visual Arts, Nashville, TN.
"White Rain," Galerie Lelong, New York, NY.
"Spring Snow," Julie Saul Gallery, New York, NY.
"Petah Coyne," Byron C. Cohen Gallery for Contemporary Art, Kansas City, MO.

Untitled #1232 (Party Girl), 2006–07
Silk flowers, feathers, silk/rayon velvet, tree branches, tassels, specially formulated wax, pigment, chicken wire, metal wire, pearl-headed hatpins, metal hardware, enamel spray paint, fabricated steel understructure, cable, cable nuts
93 x 48 1/4 x 24 1/4 inches (236.2 x 122.5 x 61.6 cm)
Private Collection

"Petah Coyne: Fairy Tales, Sculpture and Related Photographs," Robert and Elaine Stein Galleries, Wright State University, Dayton, OH.

1999
"Petah Coyne: Fairy Tales," Butler Gallery, Kilkenny Castle, Kilkenny, Ireland.

1998
"Fairy Tales," Galerie Lelong, New York, NY.
"Monastic Sightings: Buddhists on the Move," Photography Gallery, Fine Arts Center Galleries, University of Rhode Island, Kingston, RI.
"black/white/black," Corcoran Gallery of Art, Washington, DC. Traveled to High Museum of Art, Atlanta, GA.
"Petah Coyne: Photographs," Laurence Miller Gallery, New York, NY. Traveled to Weatherspoon Art Gallery, University of North Carolina, Greensboro, NC.

1996
"Photographs," Laurence Miller Gallery, New York, NY.

1994
"Petah Coyne: Recent Sculpture," Jack Shainman Gallery, New York, NY.

1992
"Petah Coyne," Cleveland Center for Contemporary Art, Cleveland, OH. Traveled through 1993 to Tyler Gallery, Tyler School of Art, Temple University, Philadelphia, PA; Bates College Museum of Art, Olin Arts Center, Bates College, Lewiston, ME; Center for Contemporary Arts, Santa Fe, NM.

1991
"Petah Coyne: Recent Sculpture," Diane Brown Gallery, New York, NY.
"Petah Coyne: Recent Work," Jack Shainman Gallery, New York, NY.
"Installation by Petah Coyne," Art Gallery, Southeastern Massachusetts University, North Dartmouth, MA.

1989
"Untitled Installation: A Grand Lobby Project," Brooklyn Museum, Brooklyn, NY.
"Recent Sculpture," Jack Shainman Gallery, New York, NY.

1988
"Petah Coyne: 1987 Augustus Saint-Gaudens Fellow," Picture Gallery, Saint-Gaudens National Historic Site, Cornish, NH.

1987
"Petah Coyne: Artist in Residence 1987," Sculpture Center, New York, NY.
"Special Projects," P.S.1, The Institute for Art and Urban Resources, Long Island City, NY.

Selected Group Exhibitions

2008
"Damaged Romanticism: A Mirror of Modern Emotion," Blaffer Gallery, University of Houston, Houston, TX. Travels through 2009 to Grey Art Gallery, New York University, New York, NY; and The Parrish Art Museum, Southampton, NY.
"Roots & Ties II," Untitled [ArtSpace], Oklahoma City, OK.

2007
"Contemporary and Cutting Edge: Pleasures of Collecting, Part III," Bruce Museum, Greenwich, CT.
"New at the Nasher," Nasher Museum of Art, Duke University, Durham, NC.
"Passion Complex: Selected Works from the Albright-Knox Art Gallery," 21st Century Museum of Contemporary Art, Kanazawa, Japan.
"Shadow," Galerie Lelong, New York, NY.
"Uncontained," Whitney Museum of American Art, New York, NY.
"Back to the Future: Contemporary Art from the Mead Collection," Mead Art Museum, Amherst College, Amherst, MA.

2006
"Material Actions," Museum of Contemporary Art San Diego, San Diego, CA.
"ARS 06: Sense of the Real," Museum of Contemporary Art Kiasma, Helsinki, Finland.
"3D - An Exhibition of Contemporary Sculpture," Carl Solway Gallery, Cincinnati, OH.
"Art on the Edge: Modern & Contemporary Art from the Permanent Collection," Joslyn Art Museum, Omaha, NE.
"Waxworks," Silvermine Guild Arts Center, New Canaan, CT.
"In Focus: 75 Years of Collecting American Photography," Addison Gallery of American Art, Andover, MA.

2005
"The Forest: Politics, Poetics and Practice," Nasher Museum of Art, Duke University, Durham, NC.
"Neo-Baroque!" Byblos Art Gallery, Verona, Italy.
"Nine Contemporary Sculptors: Fellows of the Saint-Gaudens Memorial," UBS Art Gallery, New York, NY.

2004
"American Art: Selections from the Permanent Collection 1900–1960," Weatherspoon Art Museum, Greensboro, NC.
"Ten," Byron C. Cohen Gallery for Contemporary Art, Kansas City, KS.
"Bodily Space: New Obsessions in Figurative Sculpture," Albright-Knox Art Gallery, Buffalo, NY.
"Revelation: A Fresh Look at Contemporary Collections," The Mint Museum, Charlotte, NC.
"Behind Closed Doors," Katonah Museum of Art, Katonah, NY.

Untitled #1181 (Dante's Daphne), 2004–06
Rayon and silk flowers, fabricated tree branches, berries, feathers, artificial birds, specially formulated wax, silk/rayon velvet, nylon thread, chicken wire fencing, wire, cable, shackles, pearl-headed hatpins, black spray paint, metal tubing, metal wire, cable nuts
62 x 70 x 101 inches
(157.5 x 177.8 x 256.5 cm)

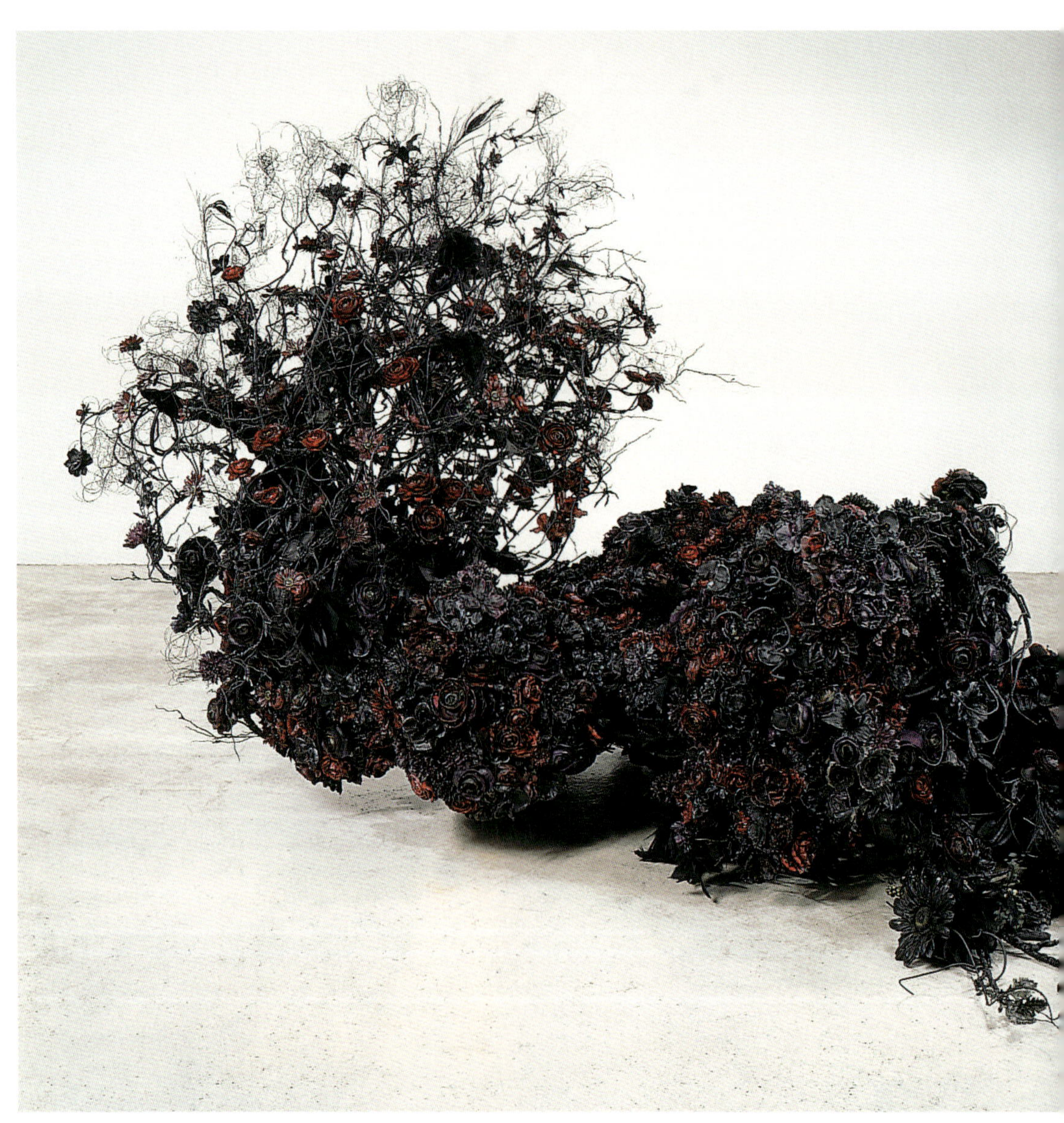

"The Print Show," Exit Art, New York, NY.
"Birdspace: A Post-Audubon Artists Aviary," Contemporary Arts Center, New Orleans, LA. Traveled to Norton Museum of Art, West Palm Beach, FL; and Hudson River Museum, Yonkers, NY.

2003
"Materials, Metaphors, Narratives: Work by Six Contemporary Artists," Albright-Knox Art Gallery, Buffalo, NY.
"Visions and Revisions: Art on Paper Since 1960," Museum of Fine Arts, Boston, MA.
"Cold Comfort," Memphis College of Art, Memphis, TN.

2002
"Petah Coyne/Ann Hamilton," Des Moines Art Center, Des Moines, IA.
"Shift," Galerie Lelong, New York, NY.
"Into the Woods," Julie Saul Gallery, New York, NY.
"Flat Not Flat: Four Sculptors Confront the Wall," Judy Ann Goldman Fine Art, Boston, MA.
"Eve and the Snake," Kunstverein Bad Salzdetfurth e.V., Bodenburg, Germany.
"Feminism and Art: Selections from the Permanent Collection," National Museum of Women in the Arts, Washington, DC.
"What's Hot and New in 2002: A Print and Photography Exhibition and Sale," Katonah Museum of Art, Katonah, NY.
"Time Distance Memory," Laurence Miller Gallery, New York, NY.

2001
"Artists Take On Detroit: Projects for the Tricentennial," Detroit Institute of Arts, Detroit, MI.
"Lateral Thinking: Art of the 1990s," Museum of Contemporary Art San Diego, La Jolla, CA. Traveled through 2004 to Colorado Springs Fine Arts Center, Colorado Springs, CO; Hood Museum of Art, Dartmouth College, Hanover, NH; Dayton Art Institute, Dayton, OH.

2000
"Snapshot: An Exhibition of 1,000 Artists," Contemporary Museum, Baltimore, MD.
"SCULPTography," Galerie Lelong, New York, NY.
"The Glen Dimplex Artists Award 2000," Irish Museum of Modern Art, Dublin, Ireland.
"Whitney Biennial 2000," Whitney Museum of American Art, New York, NY.
"Muscle: Power of the View," Boulder Museum of Contemporary Art, Boulder, CO.
"The End: An Independent Vision of Contemporary Culture, 1982–2000," Exit Art, New York, NY.
"Faith: The Impact of Judeo-Christian Religion on Art at the Millennium," Aldrich Contemporary Art Museum, Ridgefield, CT.
"Rapture," Bakalar and Huntington Galleries, Massachusetts College of Art and Design, Boston, MA.

1999
"Photographs by Painters, Photographers, Sculptors," Lennon, Weinberg, Inc., New York, NY.
"Object Lessons: Selections from the Robert J. Shiffler Foundation," Columbus Museum of Art, Columbus, OH.
"Millennium Messages," Heckscher Museum of Art, Huntington, NY. Traveled through 2001 to Tufts University Art Gallery, Tufts University, Medford, MA; Everson Museum of Art, Syracuse, NY; and Miami University Art Museum, Oxford, OH.
"Best of Season: Selected Work from the 1998–1999 Manhattan Exhibition Season," Aldrich Contemporary Art Museum, Ridgefield, CT.
"Surroundings: Responses to the American Landscape, Selections from the Permanent Collection of the Whitney Museum of American Art," San Jose Museum of Art, San Jose, CA.
"Drawing in the Present Tense," Aronson and Main Galleries, Parsons School of Design, New York, NY. Traveled through 2000 to Julian Akus Gallery, Eastern Connecticut State University, Willimantic, CT; North Dakota Museum of Art, Grand Forks, ND.
"Souvenirs/Documents: 20 years," P.S. 122, New York, NY.
"Domestic Pleasures," Galerie Lelong, New York, NY.

1998
"Coming Off the Wall," Susquehanna Art Museum, Harrisburg, PA.
"Connections & Contradictions: Modern and Contemporary Art from Atlanta Collections," Michael C. Carlos Museum, Emory University, Atlanta, GA.
"The Human Habit," William King Regional Arts Center, Abingdon, VA.
"Selections from the Permanent Collection," Museum of Contemporary Art San Diego, La Jolla, CA.
"Masters of the Masters: MFA Faculty of the School of Visual Arts, New York 1983–1998," Butler Institute of American Art, Youngstown, OH.
"House of Wax," The Contemporary Arts Center, Cincinnati, OH.
"Sculptors and their Environments," Pratt Institute Manhattan Gallery, New York, NY. Traveled to Rubelle & Norman Schafler Gallery, Pratt Institute, Brooklyn, NY.
"Preview, Review," Galerie Lelong, New York, NY.

1997
"Eye of the Beholder: Photographs from the Avon Collection," International Center of Photography, New York, NY.
"Selections from the Collections," Museum of Modern Art, New York, NY.
"Biennial Exhibition of Public Art," Neuberger Museum of Art, Purchase College, State University of New York, Purchase, NY.

"Partners in Printmaking: Works from Solo Impression," National Museum of Women in the Arts, Washington, DC.

1996

"Simple Gifts: A Selection of Gifts to the Collection from Lily Auchincloss," Museum of Modern Art, New York, NY.

"Transforming the Social Order," Temple Gallery, Tyler School of Art, Temple University, Philadelphia, PA.

"Inside," California Center for the Arts, Escondido, CA.

"Graphics from Solo Impression Inc.," Members' Gallery, Albright-Knox Art Gallery, Buffalo, NY.

"Square Bubbles," Mandeville Gallery at the Nott Memorial, Union College, Schenectady, NY.

1995

"The Invisible Force: Nomadism as Art Practice," Polk Museum of Art, Lakeland, FL.

"Inside/Outside: From Sculpture to Photography," Laurence Miller Gallery, New York, NY.

"Essence and Persuasion: The Power of Black and White," Anderson Gallery, University of Buffalo, State University of New York, Buffalo, NY.

"Other Choices/Other Voices," Islip Art Museum, East Islip, NY.

"Object Lessons: Feminine Dialogues with the Surreal," Massachusetts College of Art and Design, Huntington Gallery, Boston, MA.

1994

"Prints from Solo Impression Inc.," The College of Wooster Art Museum, The College of Wooster, Wooster, OH.

"Fabricated Nature," Boise Art Museum, Boise, ID. Traveled to University of Wyoming Art Museum, University of Wyoming, Laramie, WY; Virginia Beach Center for the Arts, Virginia Beach, VA.

"The Garden of Sculptural Delights," Exit Art / The First World, New York, NY.

"In the Lineage of Eva Hesse," Aldrich Contemporary Art Museum, Ridgefield, CT.

1993

"Drawings: 30th Anniversary Exhibition," Leo Castelli Gallery, New York, NY.

"25 Years, A Retrospective," Cleveland Center for Contemporary Art, Cleveland, OH.

"Monumental Propaganda," Courtyard Gallery, World Financial Center, New York, NY. Traveled through 1998 to International Gallery, Smithsonian Institution, Washington, DC; Dunlop Art Gallery, Regina Public Library, Saskatchewan, Canada; Muckenthaler Art Center, Fullerton, CA; Bass Museum of Art, Miami Beach, FL; Kemper Museum of Contemporary Art, Kansas City, MO; Helsinki City Art Museum, Helsinki, Finland; Lenin Museum, Tampere, Finland; Uppsala Konstmuseum, Uppsala, Sweden;

Contemporary Art Center, Copenhagen, Denmark; Kennesaw State University, Kennesaw, GA; Organized by Independent Curators International.
"Forest of Visions," Knoxville Museum of Art, Knoxville, TN. Traveled to Cheekwood Museum of Art, Nashville, TN; Samuel P. Harn Museum of Art, Gainesville, FL.
"Testwall," TZ'Art & Co., New York, NY.

1992
"Miauhaus," Thread Waxing Space, New York, NY.
"Beauty and the Beast," Neuberger Museum of Art, Purchase College, State University of New York, Purchase, NY. Traveled to Artists Space, New York, NY.
"Natural Forces / Human Observations," Charlotte Crosby Kemper Gallery, Kansas City Art Institute, Kansas City, MO.

1991
"Contemporary Collectors," Museum of Contemporary Art San Diego, La Jolla, CA.
"Vital Forces: Nature in Contemporary Abstraction," Heckscher Museum, Huntington, NY.
"10th Annual Awards in the Visual Arts," Hirshhorn Museum and Sculpture Garden, Smithsonian Institution, Washington DC. Traveled through 1992 to Albuquerque Museum of Art, History and Science, Albuquerque, NM; Toledo Museum of Art, Toledo, OH; The BMW Gallery, New York, NY.

1990
"Visions 90, in Art Contemporain 1990," La galerie d'art lavalin in collaboration with Centre international d'art contemporian de Montreal, Montreal, Quebec, Canada.
"Detritus: Transformation and Re-Construction," Jack Tilton Gallery, New York, NY.
"The (Un) Making of Nature," A two-part exhibition at Whitney Museum of American Art at Phillip Morris, New York, NY and Whitney Museum of American Art Downtown at Federal Reserve Plaza, New York, NY. Traveled to Whitney Museum of American Art at Fairfield County, Stamford, CT.
"American Academy and Institute of Arts and Letters Invitational Exhibition of Painting and Sculpture," American Academy and Institute of Arts and Letters, New York, NY.
"Visiting Artist Exhibition," Edwin W. Zoller Gallery, School of Visual Arts, Pennsylvania State University, University Park, PA.

1989
"Terra Firma: Land and Landscape in Art of the 1980s," Wallach Art Gallery, Columbia University, New York, NY.
"Lines of Vision: Drawings by Contemporary Women," Hillwood Art Gallery, C.W. Post Campus, Long Island University, Brookville, NY. Traveled to

Blum Helman Gallery, Warehouse Space, New York, NY; Murray State University, Murray, KY; Grand Rapids Art Museum, Grand Rapids, MI; University Art Gallery, University of North Texas, Denton, TX; Richard F. Brush Gallery, St. Lawrence University, Canton, NY; University of Oklahoma, Museum of Art, Norman, OK.
"The Emerging Figure," Norton Museum of Art, West Palm Beach, FL. Traveled to The Edith C. Blum Art Institute, Milton and Sally Avery Arts Center, Bard College, Annandale-on-Hudson, NY.

1988
"Life Forms: Contemporary Organic Sculpture," Freedman Gallery, Albright College, Reading, PA.
"Primitive Works for Public Spaces: Drawings, Maquettes and Documentation for Unrealized Public Artworks," RC Erpf Gallery, New York, NY.
"Strike: Nature, Abstraction, Aggression," Valencia Community College, East Campus, Orlando, FL.
"Nomadic Visions: Recent Works by Six New York Sculptors," Art Gallery, Southeastern Massachusetts University, North Dartmouth, MA.

1987
"Elements: Five Installations," Whitney Museum of American Art at Equitable Center, New York, NY.
"Sculpture," Proctor Art Center, Bard College, Annandale-on-Hudson, NY.
"O.I.A. Tenth Anniversary Outdoor Sculpture Exhibition," Snug Harbor Cultural Center, Staten Island, NY.
"Personal Poetics," Sala 1, Rome, Italy.
"Alternative Supports: Contemporary Sculpture on the Wall," David Winton Bell Gallery, Brown University, Providence, RI.
"Standing Ground: Sculpture by American Women," Contemporary Arts Center, Cincinnati, OH.
"Group Show," Grand Street Gallery, New York, NY.

1986
"A Contemporary View of Nature," Aldrich Contemporary Art Museum, Ridgefield, CT.
"South Beach III-Outdoor Public Sculpture," Organization of Independent Artists, Staten Island, NY.
"The Figure Abstracted: Intimated Presences," Robeson Center Gallery, Rutgers University, Newark, NJ.
"Sydney Blum/Petah Coyne/Beverly Fishman," P.S. 122, New York, NY.
"Transformations," Richard Green Gallery, New York, NY.
"Nature Observed: Sculpture, Painting and Photography by Contemporary Artists," Danforth Museum of Art, Boston, MA.
"The All Natural Disaster Show," P.S. 39 Longwood Art Project, Bronx, NY.
"Bodies and Dreams," White Columns, New York, NY.
"Sculpture X Six," Bronx Museum of

the Arts, Satellite Gallery, Hostos Community College, Bronx, NY.
"Group Show," Stokker/Stikker Gallery, New York, NY.
"Small Works," Sculpture Center, New York, NY.

1985
"Bayou Show," The Houston Festival, Houston, TX.
"Getting Off," Civilian Warfare, New York, NY.

1984
"Drawings," Sculpture Center, New York, NY.
"Sculpture Chicago '84," Sculpture Chicago '84, Chicago, IL.
"Holiday Invitational," A.I.R. Gallery, New York, NY.

Monographs

Lloyd, Ann Wilson. *Petah Coyne: Vermilion Fog.* Milan: Edizioni Charta, 2008.
Dreishpoon, Douglas, Eleanor Heartney and Nancy Princenthal. *Petah Coyne: Above and Beneath the Skin.* Buffalo, New York: Albright-Knox Gallery, 2005.
Princenthal, Nancy. *Petah Coyne: Fairy Tales.* Kilkenny, Ireland: The Butler Gallery, 1999.
Dreishpoon, Douglas. *Petah Coyne: Photographs.* New York: Laurence Miller Gallery, 1996.
Sultan, Terrie and Carrie Przybilla. *Petah Coyne: black/white/black.* Washington, DC: The Corcoran Gallery of Art, 1996.
Rubin, David S. *Petah Coyne.* Cleveland: Cleveland Center for Contemporary Art, 1992.
Antonsen, Lasse. *Installation by Petah Coyne.* North Dartmouth, MA: Southeastern Massachusetts University, 1991.

Selected Awards

Anonymous Was A Woman, Artist Grant, New York, NY, 2007.
Civitella Ranieri Center, Visual Arts Fellowship, Umbertide, Italy, 2005.
Honorary Doctorate, Art Academy of Cincinnati, Cincinnati, OH, 2001.
Museum of Modern Art, Glen Dimplex Award Finalist, Dublin, Ireland, 2000.
Sirus Project, Cobh Fellowship, County Cork, Ireland, 2000.
AICA International Association of Art Critics, Exhibition Award, 1999.
The Joan Mitchell Foundation, Sculpture Grant, New York, NY, 1998.
Acadia Art Program Fellowship, Northeast Harbor, ME, 1997.
AICA International Association of Art Critics, Exhibition Award, 1995.
National Endowment for the Arts, International Exchange, US/Mexico Creative Artists' Residency Grant, 1994.
Asian Cultural Council, Japan Fellowship, New York, NY, 1992/93.
National Endowment for the Arts, Sculpture Fellowship, Washington, DC, 1990.
National Endowment for the Arts, International Exchange Fellowship, France, 1990.
Awards in the Visual Arts, Southeastern Center for Contemporary Art. Winston-Salem, NC, 1990.
The Rockefeller Foundation, Bellagio Residency Fellowship, Italy, 1990.
John Simon Guggenheim Memorial Foundation, Fellowship, New York, NY, 1989.
Art Matters, Inc. Artist Grant, New York, NY, 1989.
New York Foundation for the Arts, Sculpture Fellowship, New York, NY, 1988.
Massachusetts Council on the Arts and Humanities, New Works Grant, Boston, MA, 1988.
Pollock-Krasner Foundation, Inc. Artists Grant, New York, NY, 1988.
Augustus Saint-Gaudens Memorial Foundation, Sculpture Fellowship, Cornish, NH, 1987.
Artists Space, Committee for the Visual Arts, Inc., New York, NY, 1984, 1986, 1987.

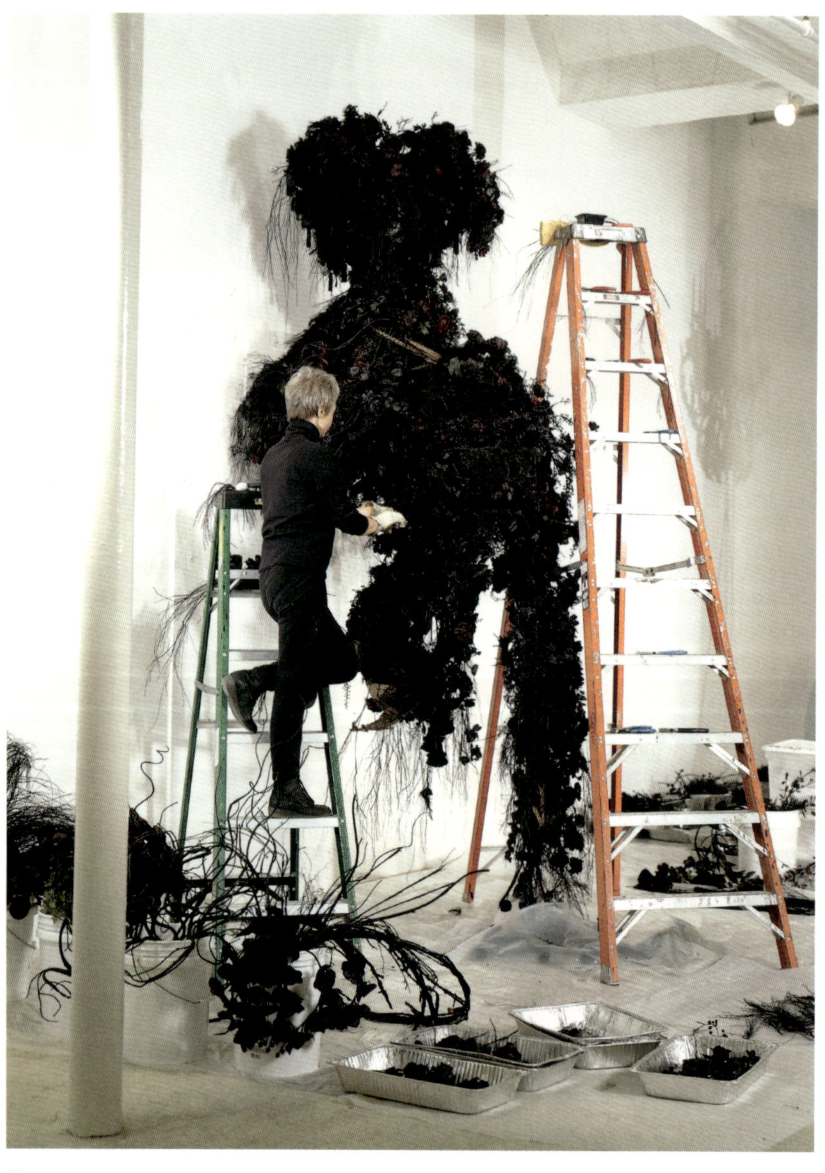

The artist in her studio, West New York, New Jersey, 2004

Public Collections

Addison Gallery of American Art, Phillips Academy, Andover, MA.
Albright-Knox Art Gallery, Buffalo, NY.
Art Museum of Western Virginia, Roanoke, VA.
Avon Products, Inc., New York, NY.
Bell Atlantic, Cincinnati, OH.
Brooklyn Museum, Brooklyn, NY.
Brooklyn Union Gas, Brooklyn, NY.
Cincinnati Art Museum, Cincinnati, OH.
Corcoran Gallery of Art, Washington, DC.
Des Moines Art Center, Des Moines, IA.
Detroit Institute of Arts, Detroit, MI.
High Museum of Art, Atlanta, GA.
Hirshhorn Museum and Sculpture Garden, Smithsonian Institution, Washington, DC.
Joslyn Art Museum, Omaha, NE.
Kemper Museum of Contemporary Art, Kansas City, MO.
List Visual Arts Center, Massachusetts Institute of Technology, Cambridge, MA.
Mead Art Museum, Amherst College, Amherst, MA.
Metropolitan Museum of Art, New York, NY.
Mint Museum of Art, Charlotte, NC.
Morgan Stanley, New York, NY.
Museum of Contemporary Art, North Miami, FL.
Museum of Contemporary Art Kiasma, Helsinki, Finland.
Museum of Contemporary Art San Diego, San Diego, CA.
Museum of Fine Arts, Boston, MA.
Museum of Modern Art, New York, NY.
Nasher Museum of Art, Duke University, Durham, NC.
National Museum of Women in the Arts, Washington, DC.
Nelson-Atkins Museum of Art, Kansas City, MO.
Neuberger & Berman, New York, NY.
New School for Social Research, New York, NY.
Phoenix Art Museum, Phoenix, AZ.
Progressive Corporation, Cleveland, OH.
Solomon R. Guggenheim Museum, New York, NY.
Speed Art Museum, Louisville, KY.
Spencer Museum of Art, University of Kansas at Lawrence, Lawrence, KS.
Weatherspoon Art Gallery, University of North Carolina, Greensboro, NC.
West Collection, Oaks, PA.
Whitney Museum of American Art, New York, NY

Design
Gabriele Nason, Daniela Meda

Editorial Coordination
Filomena Moscatelli

Copyediting
Charles Gute

Copywriting and Press Office
Silvia Palombi Arte&Mostre, Milano

US Editorial Director
Francesca Sorace

Promotion and Web
Monica D'Emidio

Distribution
Antonia De Besi

Administration
Grazia De Giosa

Warehouse and Outlet
Roberto Curiale

Cover
Untitled #1180 (Beatrice), *2003–08*
detail

ISBN 978-88-8158-684-4

Printed in Italy

Photo Credits
All photography by Wit McKay unless noted previously.
All images Courtesy Galerie Lelong, New York, unless otherwise noted.

Edizioni Charta srl
Milano
via della Moscova, 27 - 20121
Tel. +39-026598098/026598200
Fax +39-026598577
e-mail: edcharta@tin.it

Charta Books Ltd.
New York City
Tribeca Office
Tel. +1-313-406-8468
e-mail: international@chartaartbooks.it
www.chartaartbooks.it

Published on the occasion
of Petah Coyne's exhibition
Vermilion Fog at Galerie Lelong, New York
October 24 – December 6, 2008

Galerie Lelong
528 West 26th Street
New York, NY 10001
www.galerielelong.com

The artist wishes to thank:
Mary Sabbatino, Mark Hughes,
Lindsay Macdonald, Wade Miller,
Stephanie Joson, Bridget Donlon,
Douglas Breismeister, Robin McKay,
Lucienne Pereira, Monique Luchetti,
Elissa Goldstone, Gail Biederman,
Steven Millar, Ed Reilly, Tricia Townes,
Elisabeth Bernstein, Nyna Mezan,
Allison Brainard, Amanda Katz,
Jenna Rosenberg, Gary Petersen,
Kenneth Short, Nils (Kerry) Wessell,
Libby Rothfeld, Silvana Davila,
Merry Conway, Noni Pratt,
Arthur Gibbons, Kenji Fujita,
Laurence Hegarty, Donald Porcaro,
DeWitt Godfrey, Mike Asente,
Ann Wilson Lloyd, Leslie Scalapino,
Wit McKay, John Dilsizian,
David Shirey, Kathleen McCarthy,
Anonymous Was a Woman,
Ron and Linda Daitz,
and, far from last, Lamar Hall.

To find out more about Charta, and to learn about our most recent publications, visit

www.chartaartbooks.it

Printed in July 2008
by Tipografia Rumor srl, Vicenza
for Edizioni Charta